Mission Statement

Children's Historical Publishing empowers children, especial integrating art, history, science and technology into product educational experience.

Published by: Children's Historical Publishing

Founder: William F. Bell 1998
Executive Director: Joyce Kasprzak
Contact us at (937)643-0502 or at www.chpsbooks.org

Joyce Kasprzak	Brian Reid	Kim Villalva	Kathleen Russell
Executive Director	Editor	Author	Graphic Design

Teacher's Curriculum Guides available for free download at:
www.chpsbooks.org

Special thank you to our Contributors:
Margaret Kruckemeyer

OH CARES

Thank you to friends and supporters of Children's Historical Publishing whose dedicated efforts and input have helped complete this project.

Introduction

Not long ago, I was observing my 90-year-old mother have a conversation with my young female cousin. My cousin was preparing to graduate from high school, and my mother was asking her what she planned to do after graduation. Not really giving my cousin much time to answer the question, my mother launched into all the potential careers available to my cousin, careers that included astronaut, engineer, pilot, doctor, lawyer and mathematician. My cousin patiently sat and listened to my mother. I'm sure she was wondering why it was so important for my mother to offer this detailed list.

From my mother's perspective, it was incredibly important for her to offer this list, because it would have been markedly different 50 years ago. She in fact was EMPOWERING my young cousin to make a choice to make a difference in the world. The important part of the conversation was that there were no limits to the list and to the potential for my cousin. As an observer, I found myself smiling both inside and out as I saw a female from the Greatest Generation offering valuable advice to a female Gen Z'er, which was rooted in many years of experience.

My mother and her generation, as well as the ladies that came before and after, earned the right to offer advice to young ladies. They built the bridges that we all currently walk on and forged a very sound structure, which we continue to build. Although my mother did not serve in the military, she easily could have. She chose instead to serve her country in a different way as a schoolteacher for 45 years.

The women we meet in *Empowered Women: Ohio Women in the Military* made the noble choice to serve their country, even when it was unacceptable for women to serve in the military. Some of them served right next to their husbands, some had to hide their gender to serve and others bravely took the steps to be the first to achieve a major milestone. There are many firsts highlighted in this book. Please take note of all of them and reflect on the courage required to be the first. I hope that you also take time to enjoy the resources for further learning and study at the end of the book.

My military service spans the 20th and 21st century. Throughout my service, I was continually reminded of those ladies who went before me that gave my female peers and myself the ability to choose any career that we wanted. I was blessed to serve during the time when our country saw its first female four-star general, our first female fighter pilot, our first female Army Ranger School graduate, our first female in combat and our first female to serve on a submarine.

Cassie B. Barlow, PhD,
Col (ret), USAF

The message in *Empowered Women: Ohio Women in the Military* is for all young people who are chasing their dreams. You are empowered to chase your dreams because of the sacrifice of those who came before you. Your mission, if you choose it, is to build the bridge and the strong foundation for the next generation so they can follow proudly in your footsteps.

Godspeed!

Cassie B. Barlow, PhD, Col (ret), USAF

Author's Note

Kim Villalva

Why read about women in the military? You don't have to want to join the military, or even have family who served, in order to find yourself on an amazing journey with the women you will read about in this book. What you will find in these true stories are examples of women who made a difference in the lives of other women, and in our country. At the end of each chapter, "Women on the Empowerment Journey" highlights special stories of women from each war.

As I researched this book and journeyed through history with these women, I found my eyes opened. I poured through several articles and books. I listened to speakers and I saw special museum exhibits. With every new story that I found, I learned about the many difficult steps that women took as they made their way into the military.

Who were these women who carved the path for others to follow? What exactly did they do? What did they learn about themselves? Soon you will learn about their powerful journey, too.

I am not the same person I was at the beginning of my writing. Reading the stories of these women has truly changed me, and for the better. Now, when I find myself getting frustrated at having to tackle something over and over, for example, I think of the women who had to *continually* prove that they, just like men, could serve. I truly am inspired by these brave women who set out to make a lasting contribution to our country by finding a place for themselves in the military.

As you read this book, you will notice a section between most chapters called *"Transformational Milestones."* Transformation is defined as the "process of being changed in form, appearance, nature or character." And a milestone is a significant event in someone's life. This is where change takes place. A woman's place in the military was constantly being transformed, right before her very eyes. Right before everyone's eyes. One steady step at a time.

You will also notice **bold** words throughout the chapters. These are great words to learn and remember because they are important to our empowered women's story. Test your knowledge at the end of the book and see what you learned!

When you reach the end of the book, you will get to read a section called, *"Profiles of Empowered Ohio Women Veterans."* Told in their own words, this is your chance to hear the voices of our women veterans, for yourself. You will hear what their military experiences meant to them, as well as the many sacrifices they made to follow their dreams.

Women have served their country since the American Revolution. That means we have 245 years of history to explore! These stories are real. They were left for you and me to discover, to learn from, and to continue. Yes, we are called to continue these stories of empowerment.

See what treasures and inspirations you may find in the pages that follow. You won't be disappointed.

Kim Villalva
Author

Table of Contents

Chapter One
Empowerment and the History of Women in the Military

A husband and wife finished placing their fast-food order. The wife asked, "Do you offer a military discount?" The cashier smiled, "Yes, we do!" He turned to the husband and said, "Thank you for your service, sir!" and then waited for him to show his **military ID card**.

Many restaurants and stores offer military discounts to **veterans**, as a way of thanking them for their service. We probably see veterans out while dining or shopping and we can take a moment to thank them in our own special way. We may shake their hands. We may write thank you cards and send them to veterans in our neighborhoods or in senior centers.

Thanking our nation's veterans is so important that our country has set aside November 11th of each year to honor those who have served in the military. Every **Veterans Day** we have several opportunities to thank our veterans. We attend parades, and stand up out of respect, waving as veterans ride by on floats decorated in red, white and blue. We attend special ceremonies in city parks and Veterans Centers around the country. We listen to veterans speak about their service, their sacrifices, and their insights.

Veterans Day Parade, Columbus Ohio.

Have you ever stopped to thank a veteran? Have you ever waved at a veteran during a Veterans Day parade? If so, who exactly did you thank? Who do you see in your mind right now--was it a man that you thanked? Or...was it a woman?

Let's hear how our fast-food story above ended. Remember that the cashier was waiting for the husband to show his military ID so he and his wife could get a military discount applied to their meal. The husband grinned and shook his head, "You've got the wrong guy." His wife smiled at the shocked cashier, pulled out *her* military ID and said, "You are very welcome. I believe you needed to see my military ID for the discount."

A woman airman serving as a member of the U.S. Air Force Security Forces.

This story is all too common as women veterans are easily overlooked in everyday life. If you think about all of the times when you thanked male veterans, just like the cashier in our story, you aren't alone. When we think of our military, we often expect that the typical service member or veteran *is* and *will* be a man. After all, men have been serving since the first days that our young country saw battle on its lands.

As time went on and the military evolved with each war, the image of our American soldier and service member changed as well. No longer do we see that just men served, but we also see that women were there too! Did you know that women have served in every conflict since the American Revolution? That means that women have been serving in the military for 245 years! Women's roles in the military have changed a lot through those years, but unfortunately, the significance of their service history has not always been fully acknowledged.

It's not that women weren't there throughout the wars and conflicts. It's not that their roles have not progressed to now match those of their male counterparts, and it's certainly not that they haven't made countless sacrifices for our country. They have done all of this and more. It's just that we haven't always realized the extent to which women served and the significant impact of their military service on our country.

From the very beginning of our country, women had to confront numerous barriers, both on the battlefield and on the home front. For women who chose to serve, their job was never easy. Not only did they faced the challenges of serving in the military, but also the challenges of serving *as a woman* in the military. Those women who made the courageous decision to serve pushed through the many barriers that stood in their way. They broke out of traditional female roles and often went against the **social norms** for their time. They had a dream to serve and skills and talents to give to our country. They were leaders. They were visionaries. They were the trailblazers who transformed they face of our American veteran today.

When we think of today's veterans, we need to expand our picture of who they are. No longer should we just see the brave men who fought in World War II, Korea, Vietnam and in the current Global War on Terror. We should see the brave women who fought and served, too.

As we explore the women throughout history who served, we see women who carved out their place in the United States Armed Forces. Our nation's history of military women is one continuous story of **empowerment**. It is the story of a journey of women, that who through struggles, hard work and perseverance, showed society who they were. Their journey also showed themselves who they were...and more importantly, who they *could* be.

Air Force Basic Trainees, Lackland Air Force Base.

380th Air Expeditionary Wing, Women's History Month.

What is **empowerment**? **Empowerment** can be defined as "the process of becoming stronger and more confident, especially in controlling your life and claiming your rights." It is also "the process of gaining freedom and power to do what you want or to control what happens to you. It is the freedom to act." Empowerment is a process that involves a series of steps or actions, taken over time, that ends with a particular result.

Guided Learning Activity to Highlight Empowerment Traits

As you read through each chapter, look for examples of empowerment. What traits do you see in the women from each war? Use a regular or digital highlighter to mark examples ofempowerment that you find. Remember, empowerment is the process of taking control of what happens to you throughout your life—look for examples of women who took action, who took risks and who knew what they wanted in life.

The stories you will read about in this book chronicle the steps to empowerment for women in the military. These stories highlight the vast accomplishments of women over time, many of whom were made by women from Ohio.

What you will see in these stories are many historic firsts for the armed services. We see women who courageously forged the path for generations of women to follow.

They haven't only forged the path for other women, however; rather, they have forged the path for *anyone* to follow—male *or* female. Any person who has a dream and who has to confront challenges—both foreseen and unforeseen—can learn from what these women accomplished.

And that includes you and me. We all face challenges in our lives. When we look to the lessons that these women throughout history left for us, we find valuable

insights into how to push beyond our own limitations and barriers in order to reach our own personal goals and dreams. The lessons are right there in the history of our women veterans. All we need to do is to discover for ourselves how applicable their stories are to our very own, even 245 years later.

As you read this book, join these women on their journeys. Pretend that you are right there with them as you explore their military history. What was it that motivated them to take the steps they did? What kept them going in the face of ongoing challenges and conflict? What did they accomplish? Let's find out.

Three women airmen serving at the U.S. Air Force Basic Training facility.

A female U.S. Air Force Technical Instructor receives thanks while serving at the U.S. Air Force Basic Training facility.

Chapter Two
Revolutionary War (1775-1783)

The story of America begins. And with it, the story of empowered military women...

In the late 1700s, Ohio was known as the Ohio Country, Ohio Territory or Ohio Valley. Ohio didn't become a state until 1803.

Most settlers traveled on foot for hundreds of miles to reach Ohio Country. How long do you think it would take you to walk from Cincinnati to Cleveland? Even the fastest drive time for this 266-mile one-way trip across the state would take you roughly four hours. To travel this route by foot? Try about 80 hours. Now imagine you are coming from an east coast city and working your way west. Just to reach Ohio would take months in the late 1700s. If the distance and terrain weren't difficult enough, severe weather, dangerous animals, a lack of available food, and sickness or injury meant that your journey would be downright treacherous.

Once settlers reached their destination, the conditions they faced were just as difficult as those they faced on their journey. A frontier land with rough terrain and thick forests, Ohio Country had numerous challenges for settlers, and women were not excluded from this difficult life. Adding to the existing demands that both men and women faced, such as clearing land to build a home, for example, women typically remained at home while their husbands often worked away for long days, weeks or months. They raised the childre, grew, found and prepared food, sewed clothing, and took care of livestock, all to take care of their family. Because other homes and neighbors were spread throughout the land, women were often left alone to care for their families. They learned to be self-sufficient.

Woman spinning yarn in a colonial kitchen.

When we look back at these early years of America, we see that the foundations were laid for vast opportunities for both men and women to create our country through new ideas and values, which would guide it as it grew. There were also several opportunities for both men and women to support and to defend our new country. These opportunities were born out of the struggle for our independence from Great Britain.

The Revolutionary War began on July 9, 1775 with the battles of Lexington and Concord. The thirteen colonies officially declared their independence from Britain on July 4, 1776.

Women in the Revolutionary War

With the onset of the Revolutionary War, women now faced a difficult and unknown future. They now had opportunities to take on different roles than what was typical for women at that time, and that included fully taking over their husband's role in the family once he left for the war.

As they supported the war for America's independence, they took on the roles that would lay the foundation for future generations of American women. For the first time in our young nation's history, women took on responsibilities that marked the beginning of their journey into the military.

Challenges for Women in the Revolutionary War

1. Serving in traditional "gender" roles only.

Every man who could fight in the war was needed on the battlefield. But in order to move an army full of fighting men from place to place and to keep that army running smoothly, there were jobs to be done that didn't include picking up a gun or firing a cannon. Clothes needed washed and mended. Food needed to be prepared. And sick and wounded soldiers needed care and treatment. Army **camps** needed more than just soldiers.

When married men went to war, wives sometimes made the decision to go with their husbands. With their husbands fighting far from home, who would provide food and safety for the family? The women who left their homes to join their husbands eventually became known as "**camp followers**."

In the army camps, the army soon realized that women had skills that the soldiers needed. And so, women did their traditional "home" duties; they cooked and cleaned for the soldiers of the camp. These women were essentially the first women to serve in the military.

Opportunities for women to serve in the military beyond cooking and cleaning were limited. They weren't officially allowed to join the army. It didn't matter what additional knowledge, skills or abilities a woman had, she was largely confined to how "work" was defined for a woman at that time.

Army Camp Followers.

For the women who did follow the camps, their challenges were ongoing. The more valuable a woman was to the camp, the more likely it was for commanding officers to grant her permission to stay on with her husband. Women had to meet certain criteria in order to work in the camps. If she was not married or could not do the jobs required of her, she was not permitted to stay. If a married woman's husband passed away, she was given a certain length of time to grieve and then she had to find a new husband. If she did not re-marry, she had to leave the camp.

Camp supplies were limited at times, and so **rations** had to be carefully given out to both the men and the women. The rations that women received in exchange for the work they did depended on what type of job they had, as well as how well they did the work.

2. Dangers and limitations of nursing.

In the military, nursing was typically done by male soldiers. It was a job that required close contact with male soldiers and in times of war, the men could be dirty, diseased, bloody and injured. At this time in our history, women and men had certain societal expectations. The idea of a woman caring for a man, a soldier, in this way was very much against the **social norms** of the time. It definitely was not considered to be acceptable work for a woman.

But all of this changed when early in the Revolutionary War in 1775, General Horatio Gates asked for a woman to take care of his wounded soldiers. General George Washington then asked Congress to allow nurses to care for the men.

A plan was then created to recruit female nurses. As women had been caregivers in the home, the army saw them as a natural fit to care for wounded soldiers from the battlefield. The army frequently recruited its nurses from the camp followers. This also meant that male nurses could now focus on fighting.

Unfortunately, while women did receive low pay for their nursing work, this wasn't the only challenge they faced in their new role. Women nurses were also exposed to deadly diseases and fevers that ran rampant through the camps.

3. Not allowed to join the military.

The Revolutionary War needed every soldier who could fight on the battlefield. And yet, soldiers at that time were only defined as men. Women were not allowed to join the military.

But this rule didn't stop some women. Despite resistance that often came from all sides—from the military, from men, and from society as a whole—women still found ways to serve their country as soldiers. They simply were not content to serve within the confines of the camps by just cooking and cleaning. They also wanted to do more than to just work in nursing.

So what did they do? They broke out of their traditional gender roles. Some women decided to join in the fight at the frontlines; but in order to do so, they pretended to be men so they could pose as soldiers. Remember how families were often left struggling for food and supplies once the husbands left for battle? Some women, both married and unmarried, and often times women who were poor, enlisted in the army as men, so they could get a paycheck and provide for their families. Other women were motivated to fight as men simply because they wanted to help fight for America's independence.

One soldier who joined the fighting went by the name, Robert Shurtleff. "Robert" was actually a woman named Deborah Sampson. Deborah disguised herself as a man in order to enlist in General Washington's army in 1782. She cut her hair and took on the name, Robert. She wore men's clothing and went about her work just as any soldier would without anyone guessing she was a woman!

Deborah Sampson (left) in woman's clothing. In the photo on the right, she, as Robert Shurtleff, delivered a letter to General George Washington. She was the first woman to serve in the U.S. military. She was 21 years old.

Deborah was wounded twice while serving as a soldier and even after she recovered from her wounds, she again took on additional assignments. The third time she was wounded, she was discovered to be a woman, and then was **honorably discharged**.

Deborah Sampson wasn't the only woman who served as a man in the Revolutionary War. How many served? The exact number of women who served as men are unknown. Some women were discovered, like Deborah Sampson. Some women asked for their military pension after their service and so, when they applied using their true names, were found out then. Other women were discovered only after they were killed in battle.

Many women who disguised themselves as men in order to fight, survived the war and went back to their lives as women after the war was over. If they never applied for military pensions or were never wounded, they were never discovered. How many of these women's heroic deeds quietly disappeared into history?

Impact of Women in the Revolutionary War

1. Serving as spies.

There was another category of women who wanted to serve their country and they didn't necessarily want to take on the identity of a man to serve as a soldier, either. These women worked as spies who gathered and passed along intelligence. Some women spies worked in typical women's roles, like cooking and washing clothes, but for British military camps. This easily put the women spies into the right place at the right time to discover British plans for moving their troops, areas to target next and even when the British supplies ran low. Women who served as cooks, for example, took what they learned back to American camps, any time they went out to gather food.

Lydia Barrington Darragh meeting with a patriot soldier to pass on secret information.

2. Proven bravery.

While women may not have officially joined the army in the Revolutionary War, that didn't mean that their stories of bravery were any less, regardless of the position they served in. Women continued to tap into their own unique strengths in order to help support the war however they could.

In 1782, Fort Henry came under attack a second time by the British and their Native American allies. Located in the Ohio Country at the time, Fort Henry is now in modern-day Wheeling, West Virginia.

At the time of the attack, about 100 people were trapped inside the fort. Only 20 of the 100 were men of fighting age. And about 60 of those trapped were women and young children. The men ran out of gunpowder and the nearest supply was hidden in a cabin about 60 yards from the fort.

A young woman, named Betty Zane, knew exactly where in the cabin the gunpowder was stored and volunteered to get it. She was only 16 years old. Betty quickly dashed out of the fort and ran to the nearby cabin. The enemy did not fire on her, thinking that she was just a young girl leaving the fort. But, when they watched her return to the fort and saw that her apron was bulging with the gunpowder, they opened fire! She ran and made it safely back inside, allowing Fort Henry's inhabitants to continue fighting until more help could arrive.

"Heroism of Miss Elizabeth Zane" showing Elizabeth (Betty) Zane's heroic gun powder retrieval for Fort Henry.

3. *Support for soldiers.*

The women who served in the military worked in very important support roles as well. As cooks, nurses, and laundresses, they helped soldiers to stay healthy on the front lines. Regardless of the position they held, women were pivotal in supporting the war effort.

Women on the Empowerment Journey in the Revolutionary War

Margaret Corbin (1751-1800)

Margaret Corbin served in battle, but did not hide the fact that she was a woman. A camp follower, Margaret followed her husband, John Corbin, to the army when he enlisted in the First Company of the Pennsylvania Artillery. John's job was to load and fire cannons.

Margaret Corbin takes her husband's place at the cannon.

During the Battle of Fort Washington in November of 1776, Margaret's husband was killed. She was with him on the battlefield and immediately took his place at the cannon. Margaret continued firing until she was wounded herself. The battle was lost and she was captured, but then was later released. Margaret Corbin became the first woman to earn a pension for her service in the Revolutionary War.

Deborah Sampson

Remember Deborah Sampson, the woman who disguised herself as a man in order to serve in the army? She was eventually recognized for her heroism, not as a woman...*but as a soldier*. She was awarded pension for her faithful service to the country.

Betty Zane

Empowerment is about becoming confident in your abilities—young Betty did just that. She knew exactly where in the nearby cabin to look for the gunpowder.

Conclusion

These are just a handful of stories of women who, through courage and sacrifice, contributed to the war effort. Whether they were disguised as men, gathered secret information as spies, or cared for soldiers as nurses and cooks, their stories need to be told. These are the women who laid the foundation for generations of women that follow. How many more untold stories of women's bravery and sacrifice from this time in history are there? The exact number of women who served in the Revolutionary War is unknown.

The Betty Zane Memorial, located in Martins Ferry, Ohio. Photo by James Janos, 1999, Ohio County Public Library, Wheeling, WV.

In order to serve their country, women had to leave behind the safety of their traditional role in society and in the home. They risked their lives to serve, stepping into the unknown. They embarked on a journey full of hardships and risks, but one that opened the door to empowerment for those who would follow in America's bloodiest war just 80 years later, the American Civil War.

Chapter Three
American Civil War (1861-1865)

With the Revolutionary War behind them, our young nation established a new government that would hold for almost eighty years. As the tensions over slavery and states' rights grew between the northern states and southern states, the resulting conflict was the American Civil War. In April 1861, the Civil War officially began with the Battle of Fort Sumter in Charleston, South Carolina. One of the bloodiest conflicts in American history, the Civil War was often dubbed "Brother Against Brother" due to division amongst families depending on where they lived in the country—in the north or the south.

Women in the Civil War

With their families sometimes split between the North and the South, with armies marching through their cities, towns and countrysides, and with so many men joining in the fight, women were left with challenging responsibilities in the home. Similar to the social norms of the Revolutionary War years, women were expected to take care of their family and the home.

But this war opened up women's minds about the new ways in which they could serve their country. What should their proper place in society be? As women's roles during the Civil War were explored, this question became a significant step towards empowerment for women in the military, both during the war, and most definitely at the conclusion of it.

A woman's place was simply to be at home, not traveling by herself or leaving her family. And yet, there were those women who chose to fight against this social expectation of the time and follow the armies. Just like in the Revolutionary War, married women who made the decision to follow their husbands to war typically found themselves working as camp followers, serving as laundresses or cooks.

Challenges for Women in the Civil War

1. *Social class barriers.*

The impact of the Civil War was felt by all classes of women. Oftentimes, a woman's social class influenced the role she took on to serve her country. White, middle-class women in the North, including in the state of Ohio, renewed their devotion to the home front and caring for their family. This meant learning new skills and taking on new responsibilities in the home while the men were away fighting. They also supported the war effort and soldiers through **Aid Societies**.

Without men to provide for the family, many working-class white women had to find work so they could take care of their families. In the North, where industry was more common, working-class women found jobs in munitions, arsenals or in smaller shops.

Social class differences even impacted nursing. Southern white women were less accepted into this sort of work. Any kind of work (like hard labor) was usually done by slaves. In Confederate hospitals in the South, then, slave women outnumbered white women.

2. Illegal to serve in combat.

Impersonating Male Soldiers – Having to keep a secret

Imagine you are helping to bury soldiers following a battle. It is a hot July afternoon and you carry one soldier after another to his burial place. As you reach the next soldier, you look closely at him and discover that this soldier looks a little different from the rest. Despite wearing the same basic Union uniform, the soldier's features clearly reveal that it is not a man lying before you, but a woman! As you stand back up and wipe the sweat from your brow, you scan the battlefield full of fallen bodies. Could there be another woman disguised as a man who died in this battle? How many others might also be women?

This is a true story and it happened in July 1863 following the Battle at Gettysburg. It was illegal for women to serve in the military, either in the Union or the Confederacy. And yet, historians estimate that there were 400 to 750 women who served on the frontlines. Just like in the Revolutionary War, the exact numbers of women who served as men are unknown because many were never discovered to be women. If they never were found out, either through injury, death or after the war (if they survived), their secret was never revealed. How many women served? Three million soldiers fought in the Civil War, so could it be that the estimates of how many women fought on the front lines is much higher? Some historians argue that the count of women could be up to four times that number! Historians continue to discover new stories of women who kept their gender a secret so they could serve.

What is far more important than discovering exactly how many women served as male soldiers in the Civil War, is the fact that they *did* serve. Read that sentence again. *They did serve*. Every woman who disguised herself as a man in order to fight for her country has a story that <u>belongs</u> in history—in the history of our nation and in the military history of women. These women broke out of the restrictions placed on their gender at the time. They fought on the front lines. They just did it as men.

At this time in our history, women were still expected to fill traditional roles in society and fighting as a soldier in battle was not one of them. And yet, the women who chose to dress as men and fight rejected what society expected of them. Women were expected to treasure home and family. They were expected to learn how to cook and how to sew. A woman's place was certainly not to pursue the kind of life that a soldier led, travelling from place to place, living in rough and dirty conditions, and engaging in combat. For women who wanted to support the war in more of an "acceptable way" in society, they could work in Aid Societies instead.

Woman Who Fought In Civil War Beside Hubby Dies, Aged Ninety-two

RARITAN, N. J., Oct. 4.—Mrs. Elizabeth A. Niles, who, with close-cropped hair and a uniform, concealed her sex and is said to have fought beside her husband through the civil war, is dead here today, aged ninety-two.

The war call found the couple on their honeymoon. The husband, Martin Niles, joined the ranks of the Fourth New Jersey Infantry, and when the regiment left Elizabeth Niles marched beside him. She fought through many engagements, it is said, and was mustered out, her sex undiscovered. Her husband died several years after the war.

Newspaper story of woman who fought alongside of her husband.

So why, then, did some women break away from the accepted **social norms** of the time? What drove them to make that decision? Why would they risk possible social rejection for taking on such an unladylike position in society?

The reasons for why women disguised themselves as men so they could fight were varied and often similar to male soldiers. Patriotism was a leading cause as was that of simple survival. Women needed a way to support their families! Just like many of the men who volunteered came from struggling families, so did the women.

Some women wanted a change, they sought adventure and freedom from their life, and others simply wanted to stay with their husbands.

The Challenge of Disguise

Women who decided to go to war as men had the additional challenge of creating a new identity and concealing their gender.

When women went for their required Army physical examination, they usually were able to avoid being found out because physicals at that time were quick and mainly checked to make sure that the soldier wasn't lame and that he could see to shoot a gun. *Special note*: This was the last war where women were able to sneak through Army physicals in order to join as men.

When it came to appearance, women cut their hair, added dirt to their faces and dressed in the baggy, loose-fitting clothes of the time in order to conceal their bodies. Because teen boys signed up to fight too, it wasn't uncommon to see a man without a beard or mustache, or to hear a boy whose voice hadn't changed yet. In fact, while the Union army did have a minimum age of 18 for boys to sign up, they often overlooked the age and let younger boys in. So women who didn't look "manly" would have fit in easily.

Loreta Janeta Velazquez dressed as Confederate "Lieutenant Harry Buford".
She was a Confederate spy in the Civil War

So you might be wondering about sleeping, bathing and bathroom habits. Wouldn't it be fairly easy to find out that a man was actually a woman? Women did face these challenges but they were able to work around them. Soldiers frequently slept in their clothes and when they rarely bathed, they did so in their underwear. If a soldier typically kept to themselves and wasn't very social with others, it wouldn't be strange for him to sneak off to the woods to use the bathroom in private. Therefore, women were able to keep their identity a secret, even during personal moments.

When it came to learning how to handle a weapon, women were the same as many male soldiers who did not have prior military training. And women were held to the same standards as men. They learned together.

So, with their new identity and their gender concealed, women dressed as men and joined them in combat.

Frances Clayton in women's clothing.

Frances Clalin Clayton ("Jack Williams") in uniform.

When Women Were Discovered

What happened when a woman was discovered to be impersonating a man? If a woman was wounded in battle or sick, her true identity was usually found out. When a woman was discovered, she was discharged and sent home because it was illegal for her to serve in the military as a woman. Occasionally, a woman was even imprisoned for her deceit. Some women didn't let this stop them from serving though. There are several stories of women who were discovered and sent home. They actually took on new male names and joined up with another unit or regiment.

Impact of Women in the Civil War

1. *Soldiers Aid Societies.*

Soldiers Aid Societies were organizations that supported the military in several different ways. Women raised money for the troops, and also gathered food and medical supplies for soldiers. Aid Societies were prominent in Ohio cities, like Cleveland and Cincinnati. These aid societies eventually became part of the United States Sanitary Commission in 1861. The Sanitary Commission monitored the state of army camps and hospitals to help fight infections and diseases. They worked to improve hygiene, food and other health practices for the soldiers.

"Our Heroines, United States Sanitary Commission,"
in Harper's Weekly, April 9, 1864.

2. *Advancement of women's social position and Women's Rights Movement.*

Women's actions in the Civil War were an important step in their empowerment journey, especially in the case of women's rights. Women proved themselves to be useful, both on the battlefield, and off.

3. *African-American Women's Rights.*

Enslaved African-American women who ran away, as well as those who were already freed, sometimes found work in Union army camps as laundresses, nurses, and even spies. They took a valuable step towards freedom and towards their own empowerment by serving in the military. They made sacrifices. They died on the battlefield and they died from disease.

An ex-slave, named Harriet Jacobs, spoke in public about the role of African-American women in the struggle for freedom. She gave examples of many slave women's dedicated service as nurses on the battlefields.

Mary Starkey, an African-American woman from North Carolina, helped set up schools and hospitals. She also fought with Union officials to find decent homes and medical care for refugees (increasingly a population of women, children, and the elderly.) Women, like Mary, formed the Colored Women's Relief Associations to nurse and care for African-American and white Union soldiers. They also provided food and clothing to African-American refugees.

4. Spies.

Just like the women in the Revolutionary War, some women chose to serve as spies for either the Union or the Confederacy. One woman, Sarah Emma Edmonds, dressed as a man in order to serve, and then also volunteered as a spy. Even then, she kept her true gender a secret.

5. Training programs for nursing.

For the first time in our nation's history, the vast numbers of women who served as nurses were pivotal to the war effort. The Civil War was one of the bloodiest wars in America's history. The Revolutionary War showed society

Union Private "Frank Thompson", the name Sarah Emma Edmonds used while serving.

that women could serve as nurses thereby allowing for more men to fight in battles. The success of women as Civil War nurses showed society that training programs for nursing were well worth looking into for the future.

Women on the Empowerment Journey in the Civil War

Emma Miller (1828-1914)

Emma Miller and her granddaughter, 1910.

Emma Miller, known as "Little Mother of the Home," was loved by thousands of veterans who lived at Dayton's National Soldiers Home in Dayton, Ohio. In 1867, Emma Miller became the first woman employee of the National Home for Disabled Volunteer Soldiers in Dayton, Ohio. She was appointed as matron of the home. Emma spent fifty years at the Home, growing old with several of the men she had cared for in the war.

Clara Barton (1821-1912)

Called the "Angel of the Battlefield," Clara Barton was a Civil War nurse who frequently cared for wounded soldiers from both the Union and the Confederacy. In 1881, she founded the American Red Cross.

Clara Barton.

Susie Baker (1848-1912)

Susie Baker,
First African-American
Army Nurse.

Susie Baker was raised as a slave in Georgia and secretly attended schools taught by African-American women. She continued to learn from a white girl and a white boy, despite the law against educating African-Americans. After Susie found an opportunity to escape, she worked as a laundress with the First South Carolina Volunteers, the first African-American regiment in the U.S. Army. Her reading and writing skills were noticed and she was asked to teach both African-American children and adults. In 1862 Susie married Edward King and for the remainder of the Civil War, she travelled with her husband and served as a nurse for the soldiers in her husband's unit. She also worked as laundress and taught soldiers how to read and write. Susie Baker was never paid for her work.

Mary Walker (1832-1919)

Mary Walker volunteered as a nurse in 1861. In April 1864, she was captured and imprisoned by the Confederate Army. After her release later that year, she became the Acting Assistant Surgeon in the Ohio 52nd Infantry. In late 1865, she was the first and only woman to be awarded the Congressional **Medal of Honor** for Meritorious Service. *Special note:* Mary Walker's medal was withdrawn in 1917 when the criteria for the Medal of Honor changed. She continued to wear it anyway. Her Medal of Honor was eventually posthumously restored in 1977 by President Jimmy Carter.

Dr. Mary Edwards Walker, shown
wearing her Medal of Honor.

Mary Ann Ball Bickerdycke (1817-1901)

Mary Ann Bickerdyke

Mary Ann Bickerdycke, also known as "Mother" Bickerdycke, was born in Mount Vernon, Ohio. So deep was her care and love for soldiers that she searched battlefields for the wounded, even at night. Mary Ann Bickerdycke established more than 300 field hospitals for the Union Army during and after the Civil War, helped both veterans and women nurses get pensions from the government.

Harriet Tubman (approximately 1822-1913)

Harriet Tubman was a nurse, a cook, and a spy for the Union army. She led slaves to freedom using the Underground Railroad. She was also the first woman to lead a major military operation in the U.S. The Combahee River Raid rescued more than 700 slaves.

Harriet Tubman, 1870s.

Raid of Second South Carolina Volunteers, Harper's Weekly, July 4, 1863, p. 429.

Harriet Ross Tubman, later in life.

Conclusion

When the Civil War broke out, women had a strong desire to contribute. Thousands of nurses served and saved countless soldiers. Several women followed their husbands into battle to actively support the war effort. Women found a freedom that they hadn't experienced before, no matter what new job they took on.

Sometimes they paid a high price for that freedom. Large numbers of women snuck into regiments, fought on battlefields, were wounded, taken prisoner or killed in action. They left their families behind and went against what had been deemed the proper role for women.

Women in the Civil War continued the journey of empowerment set before them by their Revolutionary War ancestors. Their journey was also one of patriotism, bravery and sacrifice.

Chapter Four
Spanish-American War (April 21, 1898 – August 13, 1898)

While the Spanish-American War may have only lasted four short months, it was a historically significant war for our country. With the United States' victory over Spain, their colonial rule over Cuba was over. Additionally, America gained the Spanish territories of not only Cuba, but also Guam, the Spanish West Indies, the Philippines, and Puerto Rico. Through its involvement in the war, the United States transformed from a developing nation into a global power.

Women in the Spanish-American War

Just like in previous wars, women's roles were key to supporting the war, both on the home front, and in the war zones. In addition to raising money to provide aid and supplies to soldiers, women also made significant contributions to the war by serving as nurses and relief workers.

Challenges for Women in the Spanish-American War

1. Army hired nurses, but under contract.

Because the Army and Navy medical staffs were overwhelmed by the volume of soldiers infected by diseases, the U. S. Army was permitted to recruit female nurses under contract. However, the women would not be given military status, nor were they given equal standing in the Army. Over 1,500 women served as contract nurses.

2. Threat of disease.

Most nurses served in stateside hospitals, in camps, or on hospital ships. For those nurses who served in the very high risk hospitals in Cuba, they, especially, were under the constant threat of picking up the same highly contagious diseases as the soldiers that they were brought in to care for. Nurses' challenging work conditions in Cuba also included sanitation issues, working long hours and supply shortages, including food. One hundred fifty-three nurses died from diseases while serving.

Impact of Women in the Spanish-American War

1. First time in U.S. history that nurses were fully accepted in military hospitals.

Spanish-American War nurses served aboard the U.S. Army Hospital Ship Relief.

Women were originally limited in where they could serve. They could not serve in camps or overseas. But when yellow fever, malaria, and typhoid overwhelmed the camps, the need for additional nurses was critical. While 400 men were lost due to injuries from battle, 4,600 men were lost to disease. The women nurses provided quality care during this time and the military saw the value of their contributions to the war.

2. Active support from women's organizations.

Women also supported the war effort through various women's organizations like the Daughters of the American Revolution (DAR) and the Women's National War Relief Association (WNWRA). The WNWRA, formed in 1898, did similar work as the U.S Sanitary Commission in the Civil War.

Women on the Empowerment Journey in the Spanish-American War

Annie Oakley (1860-1926)

Have you ever heard of Annie Oakley, who was born in Darke County, Ohio? Most people probably recognize her name from Buffalo Bill's Wild West Show where she was

a sharpshooter in the show. But did you know that because of her remarkable marksmanship ability, she wrote a letter to President William McKinley offering to help train military troops for the war? Because women were not allowed to serve, her offer to help was rejected.

Annie Oakley's letter to President McKinley.

'Hon Wm. McKinley, President Dear Sir,
I for one feel confident that your good judgement will
carry America safely through without war.
But in case of such an event I am ready to place a
company of fifty lady sharpshooters at your disposal.
Every one of them will be an American and as they will
furnish their own arms and ammunition will be little if
any expense to the government.
very truly,
Annie Oakley'

Dr. Anita Newcomb McGee (1864-1940)

Dr. Anita Newcomb McGee helped recruit qualified nurses to serve in the Spanish-American War. When she became the Acting Assistant Surgeon General in the U.S. Army during the war, she was the only woman allowed to wear an officer's uniform. After the war, she worked on creating the needed legislation to give the Army Nurse Corps (ANC) permanent status; Dr. McGee became known as the founder of the Army Nurse Corps.

Ellen May Tower (1868-1898)

After first serving as a U.S. Army nurse in New York to care for soldiers who came in from the war, Ellen May Tower then volunteered to serve in Puerto Rico. Three months after she arrived in Puerto Rico, she came down with typhoid fever and died. She was the first female U.S. Army nurse to die in another country and the first woman to receive a military funeral.

Transformational Milestones – Early 1900s

The empowerment journey for women in the military did not just occur within each war that our nation fought in. Critical steps on this journey for women often occurred in between the wars. Remember that empowerment is a process that has a series of steps or actions taken in order to reach a particular result. As we have seen in the last three wars, each step women took on their journey helped not only to create a place for themselves, but also to solidify that place in the military.

While the Spanish-American War may have been short in duration, the impact that women made in the military was huge. For example, the contract nurses who served in the war made selfless sacrifices and were commended for their service. Because their dedication was evident and because they had proven themselves to be competent at the job, in 1901, the **Army Nurse Corps (ANC)** became a part of the United States Army Medical Department. This meant that the Nurse Corps would be permanent. In 1908, the Navy Nurse Corps was established.

Nurses were finally recognized as being valuable enough to be made permanent members of the military. Think back to the Revolutionary War when General George Washington first asked for nurses to care for the men. What a societal norm women were breaking back in 1775! And they continued to break through society's expectations again in the Civil War when many more women wanted to serve in the camps as nurses. Now in 1901, one hundred twenty-six years later, they finally broke through that barrier. But women in the military still had a long way to go in order to even get equal pay or rank. Would the steps they took in World War I solidify their place in the military even more? Keep reading. Their opportunities for serving are not over. And their empowerment journey is far from over.

Spanish-American War nurses with their patients.

Ellen May Tower was the first woman to receive a military funeral after she died of typhoid fever.

Chapter Five
World War I (1914-1918)

Three years after World War I began in Europe, the United States officially entered the war in April 1917. Germany, Italy and Austria-Hungary were at war with Great Britain, France and Russia. The United States joined with Great Britain and her allies.

Known today as the "Great War," this was the first time in history that fighting occurred on a global scale and with such epic proportions. President Woodrow Wilson wanted to prevent future wars like this from occurring so this war also became known as the "War to End All Wars."

World War I was pivotal because it was a war of many "firsts."

First Modern War – Technology

World War I was the first modern war with new technology that replaced the traditional warfare used in past wars. Armies now had new forms of transportation. Tanks and automobiles began to replace horses, even though cavalry units were still very much in use. New warfare technology also included machine guns, submarines, and even airplanes. All of these differences changed the way war was fought, which greatly impacted soldiers.

First Modern War – Chemical Warfare

World War I was the first (and the last) war to use chemical weapons. One of the most common chemical agents used was mustard gas, because of its yellow color. Because of their horrific nature and ability to produce mass casualties, chemical weapons have not been used since.

<u>Women in World War I</u>

With the change from traditional to modern warfare in World War I, the U.S. needed a lot of soldiers and weapons on the battlefield. This meant that women were then needed to step out of their traditional role in the home and into jobs that were usually held by men. Whether or not the country was ready to admit it, women were needed to fill jobs that men typically worked in both manufacturing and agriculture.

United States Food Administration Banners.

Women who stayed in the home contributed to the war effort as well. Women were asked to sign a pledge card, put out by the Food Administrator, that showed she would work to ensure that her family would limit their consumption of meat, wheat and fats. Whatever a woman could do to boost morale on the home front was valued. The government even encouraged Americans to grow their own food. These "War Gardens" allowed the government to send farm food to soldiers.

Just like the women who came before them, some women felt called to do more to serve their country. They supported the war effort by joining the military as nurses, ambulance drivers, and serving in various support roles. More than 33,000 women served in World War I.

Challenges for Women in World War I

1. Racial discrimination.

While many women found themselves taking on new roles in society by filling jobs that men had traditionally worked, these new opportunities to serve their country were not open to all women. Opportunities to serve were based on race.

2. Gender discrimination.

Women also faced gender inequality in the military. Combat nurses, for example, typically didn't have the same authority as men did, nor did they have full enlistment opportunities.

The newly formed Signal Corps Female Telephone Operators Unit, nicknamed the "Hello Girls," used civilian women. The bilingual women, who followed strict military protocol, worked close to the front lines in France sending messages between headquarters and the front. They demonstrated a strong work ethic, a high degree of competence working the switchboards, and bravery while serving as telephone operators. Despite their significant contributions, after the war they were denied veteran status and benefits.

The "Hello Girls," 223 U.S. women served as telephone operators in Seine, France, in 1918.

Additionally, when the war ended, several women from the Coast Guard, Navy and Marine Corps had to leave the service. Despite the proven success of using women in times of war, the military remained gender restricted. A woman's place was in the home and society still had a hard time adjusting to a woman leaving her home for the military

3. Influenza.

Over 400 nurses who served both overseas and in U.S. military hospitals during World War I died—most from influenza. At that time in our nation's history, the U.S. (and Europe) was hit by a highly contagious flu pandemic in 1918-1919. This deadly pandemic killed fifty million people worldwide.

Impact of Women in World War I

1. All classes of women could serve.

A major piece of the women's empowerment journey into the military came as a result of World War I. This was the first war that involved all classes of women. No longer were active military supporters just from the working or lower classes in society. No longer were those women who followed the military doing so just to provide their family with a paycheck or food because their husband had left to fight in the war. There was now a significant difference from previous wars in women's motivations to serve. All classes of women could now serve.

2. First time Army and Navy military nurses served overseas.

Adding to the list of firsts for World War I, this was the first time in our nation's history that Army and Navy nurses served overseas. Women still did not have rank though.

3. First time women could enlist in Navy and Marine Corps, without serving as nurses.

This was also the first time that women who were not serving as nurses were allowed to enlist in the Navy and Marine Corps. Non-nursing jobs opened up new opportunities for women to serve as ambulance drivers or even as mechanics in the war. Their work often took them to the battlefield where they would pull the wounded to safety.

Women still could not officially enlist in the Army and could only work in the Army as contract employees and civilian volunteers.

4. An opportunity – the Naval Act of 1916

The U.S. Navy needed more sailors at the beginning of World War I so recruitment was top priority. President Woodrow Wilson signed into law the Naval Act of 1916 with the goal of increasing the size of the Navy. A portion of the act that described who could serve was vague and its wording mentioned "all persons" who were capable could serve. Who exactly were "all persons?" Did this wording refer to just men? Or might *anyone* be capable of serving?

The Act was not specific and this was exactly the loophole that women needed, and it benefited both women and the Navy. So women joined the Navy as Yeomen, non-commissioned officers, and were given the title, "Yeoman (F)" with the "F" standing for "female." About 13,000 women enlisted in the Navy and Marine Corps.

The "Yeomanettes", as they quickly became referred to, were limited to clerical duties initially, but soon expanded their jobs to include mechanical work, munition work and other duties. With an increase in women taking on jobs men had done, men were now free to serve upon ships.

Navy Rear Adm. Victor Blue (left center) inspects Female Yeomen or "Yeomenettes."

5. Proven bravery.

Women who served in World War I proved their bravery time and time again, especially in dangerous situations.

Remember the "Hello Girls," who served as telephone switchboard operators in France? When an artillery shell broke a window in their building, they calmly remained at the switchboards, despite being told to head for cover. And then after their building caught on fire, they were the first to return to their positions at the switchboards.

Some nurses who served were wounded, and several died. Four Army nurses and one Red Cross nurse were awarded the Distinguished Service Cross, our nation's second highest military honor.

6. Women's Suffrage and the 19th Amendment.

Over 33,000 women served in World War I. They served across all services. They served overseas. They served in combat theaters and some even made the ultimate sacrifice.

But upon returning home, they still could not vote.

It was their proven service in the military (and in the jobs that men previously held in society that women had taken on) that directly impacted the public's opinion about women's right to vote. Women were empowered more than ever before to keep up the momentum and to fight for change. Society couldn't deny that women had proven themselves time and time again. Feelings about women's right to vote had finally changed, and that even included President Woodrow Wilson, who previously had not supported their right to vote prior to the war.

Uncle Sam ("Public Opinion") embracing nurse (American woman),
"If you are good enough for war you are good enough to vote".

President Wilson challenged the Senate in September 1918, "…Are we alone to ask and take the utmost that our women can give, service and sacrifice of every kind, and still say we do not see what title that gives them to stand by our sides in the guidance of the affairs of their nations and ours? We have made partners of the women in this war; shall we admit them only to a partnership of suffering and sacrifice and toil and not to a partnership of privilege and right?"

7. Eventual and lasting recognition.

While recognition was not always quick to be given for women's work during World War I, that didn't mean that it was forgotten. In 1977, President Jimmy Carter recognized those World War I women telephone operators (who were still alive), the "Hello Girls." It was a long journey to continually remind their country what they had done and all of that hard work paid off. They were finally recognized as Army veterans. It only took six decades.

Did you know that the story of the "Hello Girls" made such an impact on women's empowerment in the military that it was made into a musical in 2018? Their story was not forgotten and now serves to educate and inspire, all through a creative retelling through music.

Women on the Empowerment Journey in World War I

Ouida Mabel Okey (1893-1974)

Ouida Mabel Okey, of Graysville, Ohio, was one of three women from Ohio to serve in the Marine Reserves in 1918. Out of 5,000 women who applied, only two hundred women were chosen to serve in the U.S. Marine Corps in World War I.

Clara Edith Work Ayres (1880-1917)

Clara Edith Work Ayres, of Attica, Ohio, volunteered as a nurse with the Red Cross. While she was awaiting her departure to serve in France, she was killed on her ship in New York due to a weapon firing malfunction. She was the first American civilian killed in World War I, after the United States entered the war. Because her position with the Red Cross was not an official military position, Clara did not receive a military funeral.

Conclusion

World War I opened the door to empowerment for more women than ever before. Women had stepped out of the home and into men's jobs, and then proved that they could do the work. Women served in the military despite not receiving equal pay, benefits or treatment. While some women were content to return home to their traditional roles before the war, many others were now stirred to move into new and different jobs in society following the war.

It was the success that women found through their perseverance in World War I that would expand even more the many ways women would serve in World War II. Patriotism, courage, and sacrifice would again continue to find women ready to resume their empowerment journey.

Transformational Milestones – Post World War I

Empowerment for women meant taking consistent and steady steps into the military. Following World War I, another action occurred which helped to recognize that women had indeed carved out a place for themselves in the military. In 1928, women were granted admission to the **National Soldiers Homes**. The Dayton VA Medical Center, located in Dayton, Ohio, was an early National Soldiers Home.

Chapter Six

World War II, also known as the Second World War, engaged over thirty countries in a massive worldwide conflict. Many of the world's countries formed two opposing military forces, the Allies (which included many Western nations such as the USA, Great Britain, Canada, Australia, and many others) and the Axis (which included Germany, Italy, and Japan).

World War II was the largest and deadliest conflict in human history to date, resulting in between 70 to 85 million total fatalities worldwide. This truly global conflict was mainly fought within two separate combat theaters, the European combat theater and the Pacific combat theater.

Just like World War I was a war of many "firsts", so was World War II. Many new modern weapons, technologies and strategies were used in this war. Modern combat aircraft, the development and use of nuclear weapons and strategic bombing are just a few examples.

'Remember Dec. 7th!' Office of War Information poster promoting our shared purpose after Pearl Harbor.

On December 7, 1941, the United States of America woke up to a surprise attack that forever changed our country. The Japanese bombed Pearl Harbor, killing over 2,390 Americans. The next day, President Franklin Delano Roosevelt declared December 7th to be "a date that will live in infamy" and America declared war on Japan. And just three days later on December 11, 1941, Germany declared war upon the United States.

The war in Europe ended when Germany surrendered on May 7, 1945. In an effort to minimize American troop losses, President Truman authorized using atomic bombs. The United States dropped an atomic bomb on the Japanese cities of Hiroshima, and then on Nagasaki, on August 6 and 9, 1945. Over 200,000 people died. A few days later, Japan surrendered.

Women in World War II

Think back to the beginning of women's journey into the military when they became camp followers and cooked or did laundry for the men in the Army camps. They slowly moved into the field of nursing and eventually by World War I, they helped free up men for combat by taking on non-combat positions like secretarial, mechanic and other types of work that men had done before.

As our country again faced another global war, women found themselves balancing two different roles for how they could help. The 1940s was still very much a time that called for women to be steadfast in their traditional role of raising children and caring for the family.

In fact, when the United States started sending soldiers overseas, women were expected to keep the home safe and secure as they awaited their loved ones return.

With the onset of World War II, United States soldiers needed enough food and other supplies so they could do their jobs. The government created a program to limit the number of supplies that civilians could buy. Certain products were highly rationed and limited for sale and included things like canned goods, tires and food. This new rationing program was typically the woman's responsibility. She would carefully plan out her family's meals, take her ration book to the store and then use the right stamp to buy the amount of food her family was allowed.

Just like women in World War I had pledged to do everything they could to efficientlygrow food for the families, World War II women helped their families to plant about 20 million **Victory Gardens**. Those gardens produced 8 million tons of food!

In addition to women's roles in the home, many joined the workforce (like the women in World War I) and others still wanted to do more. The number of women who chose to serve in WWII significantly increased from WWI. Over 400,000 women served at home and abroad.

Challenges for Women in World War II

1. Segregation and racism.

Despite the new opportunities for women to serve, segregation and racism were still very real issues in the military. For example, the **Women's Army Corps (WAC)** did not allow African-American women to join until November 1943. However, there was a 10% limit on how many African-American women could serve. For example, if 500 white women joined, only 50 African-American women were allowed to join. Despite these limitations, this was the only choice open to African-American women at the time.

Women in the WAC even faced discrimination while training. Officers, for example, were allowed to train in integrated units, but their living areas were segregated. There were 6,250 African-American women who served in the WAAC/WAC.

2. Perception and image.

Despite the fact that women had continually been serving in the military, in one way or another, since the Revolutionary War, they were still fighting the negative perception of being involved in the military. Remember, going back to the beginning of our story, whenever a woman chose to step outside of what society expected of her, she often faced negative opinions and scowls. The same questions were asked in the 1940s. How could she leave her family? What kind of morals must she have to do something so unnatural to her gender? The military tried improve the perception of women by asking them to keep up their feminine appearance while serving. Makeup and nail polish were normal for women serving at the time.

3. Dangers while serving.

Have you ever taken a beach vacation? Or perhaps you may have lived somewhere warm and beautiful? What was the worst thing that happened to you there? Did your car break down while travelling? Did someone get sick? While nurses with the Army Nurse Corps weren't on vacation in the Philippines, the beautiful location made it an enjoyable place to serve. That is until December 7, 1941 when the Japanese bombed Pearl Harbor. Read on to find out what happened.

Just 10 hours after the bombing at Pearl Harbor, the Japanese turned their attack on Manila, in the Philippines. The nurses now had to work in a field hospital, deep in the hot jungle. Dysentery, mosquitoes and malaria, were all common threats to both the nurses and

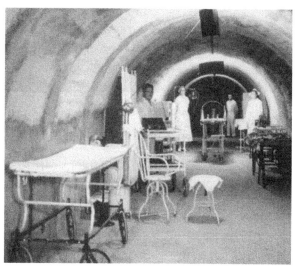

Malinta Tunnel hospital ward on Corregidor Island in 1942.

the wounded. Injured and sick soldiers were on cots outdoors. For over four months, through continued bombings and with reduced food rations, the "Angels of Bataan," as the nurses became known as, continued to do their jobs. When the fighting worsened, a makeshift hospital underground had to be created. Nurses continued caring for their patients, but were now hidden with them in the "Malinta Tunnel."

On May 6, the Japanese finally captured the Americans still on Corregidor Island in the Philippines, including 77 nurses. Gone was the paradise that the nurses had enjoyed months before. Living now under the extreme conditions of an internment camp, the nurses cared for the sick and injured in a camp hospital. **Prisoner of War (POW)** rations were cut down to just 700 calories per day and so nurses found creative ways to supplement diets with weeds and flowers.

How could the women have made it through such a challenging time? Morale stayed high. Each woman worked a daily four-hour shift. Everyone worked towards the same goal— doing their job and that of survival.

A U.S. Government Poster showing nurses from Corregidor Island.

After three years of being imprisoned, U.S. Army Nurses from Bataan and Corregidor were freed. Nurses were given new uniforms because their old clothes were worn out

In January 1945, after two and a half years of captivity, all POWs were freed, including all 77 nurses. These nurses were the first women to see combat. The path they laid would be followed again and again by the women soldiers who came after them.

Impact of Women in World War II

1. First time women served in the military in an official capacity.

165 years. Numerous wars. That's how long it took for women to finally be able to serve in the military in an official capacity. They didn't have to sneak in as men and they didn't have to stay behind as cooks or secretaries.

2. Skilled and dedicated nurses.

Over 59,000 nurses served in World War II. Their passion and dedication was so strong that even after Pearl Harbor, the Army Nurse Corps increased from 1,000 to 12,000. And their training and skill made a big difference in the survival rate of injured or ill soldiers.

A Letter to Army Nurses from Soldiers:

"To all Army nurses overseas: We men were not given the choice of working in the battlefield or the home front. We cannot take any credit for being here. We are here because we have to be.

You are here because you felt you were needed. So, when an injured man opens his eyes to see one of you, concerned with his welfare, he can't but be overcome by the very thought that you are doing it because you want to. You endure whatever hardships you must to be where you can do us the most good."

The European 'Stars and Stripes' military newspaper, October 21, 1944.

Take a moment and reflect on our military women's empowerment journey up to this point. Read the above letter a second time. The soldiers realized that nurses made a <u>choice</u> to be there…to serve, to endure hardships, to do the <u>most good</u>. When empowerment is recognized like this, it cements the progress and steps of the journey even more.

3. Rosie the Riveter.

Have you ever seen the Rosie the Riveter poster? Its bright yellow color is hard to miss. Perhaps you or someone you know has even dressed as Rosie for Halloween! Did you know that "Rosie" was based on a real woman who worked as a riveter? This powerful image of working women in World War II became a government tool to recruit women to take on the large amounts of industrial jobs the men left behind when they went to war. It became a patriotic calling for women to leave their traditional role in the home for this reason. The recruitment campaign posters worked and brought thousands of women into the work force. By 1945, one out of every four married women worked. Women only made about half of the pay that men did for the same type of work.

Rosie the Riveter, depicted in the famous U.S. Government War Production Poster.

4. Each of the military services created new organizations for women.

ARMY

WAAC recruiting postcard and poster, entitled "THIS IS MY WAR TOO!".

The Army created the Women's Army Auxiliary Corps (WAAC) in 1942 which was part of, but not fully integrated into the Army. Because of the women's success, on July 1, 1943 the name was changed to the Women's Army Corps (WAC). The WAC officially became part of the U.S. Army and gave women the rank and privileges of their male counterparts.

Fort Des Moines, the first WAAC training center in July 1942.

The WACs were the only service branch who were allowed to serve overseas and so women served stateside and in both the European and Pacific theaters. Over 150,000 women served in the Women's Army Corps.

NAVY

U.S. Navy WAVES Recruiting Poster, from 1944.

WAVES (Women Accepted for Volunteer Emergency Service) was created in July 1942. WAVES who worked stateside held the same status of naval reservists and served in communications, intelligence, and supply positions.

A group of U.S. Navy Waves during World War II.

Overseas, Navy nurses served on hospital ships and as flight nurses. Eighty thousand WAVES served in World War II.

MARINES

The Marine Corps Women's Reserves was created in 1943. Marine women served stateside as cooks, mechanics and other positions.

COAST GUARD

The Coast Guard created SPARs (their Women's Reserve) in 1943. "SPARS" stood for their motto, "Semper Paratus" which in Latin means "Always Ready." SPARs served stateside as cooks, pharmacist's mates and in other positions.

ARMY AIR FORCE

At this time, the Air Force was still a part of the Army and so it was called the Army Air Force. Have you ever wondered about the military planes that they used in the war? What happened once a plane was manufactured? How did it get from the aircraft factory to the military pilots? Imagine you are working at a busy U.S. airfield. Planes are coming and going. You are waiting for a new plane to arrive this afternoon. There it is! You spot it pulling up. It parks and you walk over to greet the pilot and to thank him for delivering the plane safely. The aircraft canopy slides open and out pops a young woman dressed in civilian garb. She is a pilot, but she is not in military uniform and she doesn't have rank—all because women were not allowed to join the Air Force. So, who is she?

Four women pilots are members of a group of WASPs, trained to ferry the B-17 'Flying Fortress' Bomber.

She is a **WASP**. She is a Women's Air Service Pilot, a civilian who worked for the Air Force. This woman would have been one of the 1,000 WASPs who served stateside during the war. These civilian women were the first women to fly military aircraft thereby freeing up male pilots for other critical roles. In addition to transporting planes, WASPs were also test pilots and helped with training missions as well. Thirty-eight WASPs lost their lives while serving.

5. Progress towards ending racial segregation and discrimination.

Empowerment is about making progress towards a goal. Noticeable steps, like the Fair Employment Practices Commission in 1941, were taken to end racial segregation and discrimination in the military. After an amendment was made to the Nurse Training Bill to stop racial bias followed in 1943, 2,000 African-Americans joined the Cadet Nurse Corps. Finally, in 1944, the quota for African- American Army and Navy nurses was eliminated. Phyllis Daley became the first African-American commissioned nurse in the Navy in 1945.

Women on the Empowered Journey in World War II

Della Raney (1912-1987)

Della Rainey seen in her Army uniform, holding the rank of Captain.

Della Raney was the first African-American woman appointed as chief nurse in the Army Nurse Corps (ANC) during World War II. She was also the first African-American chief nurse commissioned as a lieutenant in the ANC. Five hundred African-American nurses served in the ANC during WWII.

Oveta Culp Hobby (1905-1995)

Oveta Culp Hobby was appointed director of the WAAC.

Oveta Culp Hobby was the first director of Women's Auxiliary Army Corps (WAAC). She was the first woman in the Army to receive the Distinguished Service Medal, the highest non-combat award given at that time.

Charity Adams Earley (1918-2002)

Charity Adams Earley, seen at left, during her Army career, and at right, later in life.

Charity Adams Earley was the first African-American woman officer in the Woman's Army Corps. She was the commander of the 688th Central Post Battalion, the first African-American WAC unit sent overseas in WWII. By the end of WWII, Charity Adams Earley was the highest ranking African-American woman in the military, holding the rank of major. She was quoted as saying, "I just wanted to do my job."

The Charity Adams Girls Academy Elementary School is located in Dayton, Ohio.

Conclusion

From women who just wanted to do whatever they could to serve, to those who stayed strong during times of extreme wartime crisis, the women who served in World War II once again proved their bravery and steadfast service to our nation. Despite their commitment, there were significant challenges that women service members faced when the war ended.

For one, women could not continue to serve. So what was a woman to do once her service to her country was over? She had to return to civilian life and resume her role in caring for her family.

This also included women on the home front who worked the jobs men had left to go overseas. When the war ended, soldiers were **demobilized** and returned home. Hundreds of thousands of women had to give up their jobs. Can you imagine being forced to quit something you love doing? With the war over, people's attitudes about women's patriotic duty shifted once again and women were expected to return to the family. Even after showing bravery, dedication to duty and service to the Armed Forces, the war was over. So women had to step down.

Another challenge facing women after they departed from military service was that of discrimination against WASPs. Because they were civilian employees, they did not have official military status. That meant no benefits, pension or military honors for those women who died while serving. But their empowerment story was far from over. You'll have to keep reading to find out how it ends.

Despite all of the challenges women in World War II faced, their perseverance left quite an impact on their empowerment journey. Their path into the military was well underway. Where would this journey take women next? Would they have to wait for the next war to again prove themselves? Or had they done enough to show the country why they were worthy of military service? Women showed that they weren't about to be stopped by these challenges. And what happened after World War II showed everyone that women were serious about the military.

Transformational Milestones – Post World War II

April 16, 1947 – The Army-Navy Nurses Act of 1947, signed by President Harry S. Truman, established The Army Nurse Corps (ANC) as a part of the Army.

January 6, 1948 – Army First Lieutenant Nancy C. Leftenant and Navy Ensign Edith DeVoe were the first African-American women to join the Navy and Army Nurse Corps.

June 12, 1948 – The **Women's Armed Services Integration Act of 1948** allowed women to serve as permanent members of the military and they could continue serving even after a war was over.

July 26, 1948 – President Harry S. Truman signed Executive Order 9981 which abolished segregation and discrimination in the United States Armed Forces. In the five-year span from World War II to Korea, significant steps happened that changed history for women in the military. For the first time, women were allowed to be permanent members of the Army, Navy, Marine Corps and Air Force. Racial segregation was eliminated. Steps to women's empowerment were taking root.

Chapter Seven
Korean War (1950-1953)

The Korean War, which began on June 25, 1950, was the first military action of the Cold War. North Korea, a Communist nation, invaded South Korea with the intent of reuniting the two countries under Communism. The North Korean invasion prompted the United States to intervene to stop Communism from spreading in South Korea and around the world. Working with the United Nations (UN), the United States then sent military troops to free South Korea from North Korea's occupation.

North Korean troops were pushed out of South Korea, and back into North Korea, until China joined to fight with the North Koreans. Fighting eventually was pushed back to the '38th parallel' (now the current border between North and South Korea), and the war ended in a ceasefire on July 27, 1953 with South Korea remaining a free country.

Although lasting only three years, the loss of life in the Korean War was very high. Almost 5 million people died in the War, with 10% of those being civilians. America lost nearly 40,000 soldiers in the war, and that number would have been much higher without a unique battlefield concept introduced in this war, called a MASH unit (Mobile Army Surgical Hospital). Because these field hospitals followed U.S. troops in combat, they moved frequently and often ended up close to the battlefields. MASH units treated the wounded very quickly, which helped to reduce deaths from battle wounds by 50 percent compared to World War II figures.

Women in the Korean War

Remember what happened to women at the end of World War II? Troops were demobilized and returned home, so women gave up their jobs and went back to their families. Because the Korean War was much shorter than World War II, there wasn't the same need for large numbers of women to enter the civilian workforce.

Challenges for Women in the Korean War

1. Gender stereotypes and expectations.

If you have never watched an old black and white TV show from the 1950s called, "Leave it to Beaver," check it out. Mrs. June Cleaver, the mom, took excellent care of her husband and two sons, always having a healthy dinner ready on time and keeping her family strong and intact. This show was just one way that the traditional gender roles of women were reinforced in the 1950s. Women were expected to be like Mrs. Cleaver and to identify as wives and mothers, too.

Did you know that the term "nuclear family" has ties to the Cold War? Nuclear families were needed to keep our country strong; and they promoted the American way of life. And a woman's role in the nuclear family, just like that of Mrs. Cleaver, was crucial in fighting the Cold War. Communism could not win and it was a very real threat to the United States. Can you imagine the kind of pressure that many women felt who wanted to serve in the military?

Where else in our story of women's empowerment does this sound familiar? One hundred seventy-five years after women first left their homes to serve in the Revolutionary War, they are *still* being challenged by this same barrier—that of gender stereotypes. Generation after generation of women faced this challenge and the women of the Korean War were no exception.

Women who chose to serve in the Korean War served in a variety of ways—one-third were healthcare providers and others volunteered for Women's Army Corps (WAC), Women in the Air Force (WAF), WAVES, and Women Marines.

2. *Dangers of serving.*

Army Major Genevieve Smith was on her way to be Chief Nurse in the Korean theater when her plane crashed on July 27, 1950. She was the only Army nurse to be killed because of the war.

When the Navy hospital ship, the USS Benevolence, was rammed and sank in August 1950, nurses on board didn't have time to get into life boats. All they could do throughout the cold night was to hang on to pieces of the ship until the next day when they were rescued. One nurse died from shock.

After a MASH unit convoy was attacked, nurses spent the night in a ditch, speaking only in whispers while they hid from the enemy. They crawled out at dawn and cared for the wounded left on the road.

Impact of Women in the Korean War

1. *Significant and groundbreaking time for women.*

The Korean War was groundbreaking for women in that it was gender and racially desegregated. The military was now more free of barriers for women than in any previous war. In 1948, President Harry S. Truman's Executive Order 9981 eliminated racial discrimination and segregation in the United States Armed Forces. Because of the Women's Armed Services Integration Act of 1948, it was much more culturally acceptable to see women in the military. And that included African- American women. By April of 1950, WACs began integrated training and living.

For those women who served stateside, they now had more opportunities to break into nontraditional jobs. They served in positions as pharmacists, engineers, parachute riggers, air control and intelligence. When almost 3,000 women Marines took on new roles, male Marines were now free for combat duty.

> *"I learned by women serving in the military, we relieved a serviceman to execute his job to protect our country, I am so proud to have been able to serve my country in this capacity and I am still trying daily to make the Marine Corps proud of me."*
>
> **~ Daisy Losak, Marine Corps Sergeant in the Korean War,**
> **upon seeing a female Marine on a recruitment poster and deciding to join the military,**
> **just as her father and four brothers had before her.**

Korean War Era Recruitment Posters for Women.

2. Greater opportunities to serve overseas.

Only nurses could serve in the combat theater. Nurses were just days behind the first troops who landed in Korea. They also served onboard hospital ships, on the battlefield, in MASH units, in MEDEVAC aircraft, and in hospitals in Korea and Japan. In addition to caring for wounded soldiers, they also treated wounded civilians.

3. Pioneers.

Have you ever had to do a project, but not had the right tools or supplies to do it? That can be pretty stressful, especially if you are working under a deadline or other pressure. Imagine facing this type of situation; but this time, lives are at stake. As a MASH nurse, you go to the supply closet to search for anything that will work to treat your sick patients but the supplies you need just aren't there. You and your patients are in the middle of a cold winter. You are working long hours and hear artillery shells falling in the distance. When will you move again? What do you do? Nurses, like those in the 11th Evacuation Hospital in Pusan who came up with new treatment options for patients, faced similar situations and became creative problem solvers. They did their jobs because they had to, and that meant not giving up when difficulties arose.

Women on the Empowerment Journey in the Korean War

Margaret Jean Madden (1925-2013)

Margaret Jean Madden, of Franklin County, Ohio, served in the Army in the Korean War. She was the first Women's Army Corps officer from the state of Ohio to achieve the rank of Colonel. Later, she served as a charter member of the Governor's Advisory Committee on Women Veterans.

Margaret Jean Madden, later in life.

Alene Bertha Duerk (1920-2018)

Rear Admiral Alene B Duerk.

Alene B. Duerk, of Henry County, Ohio, served in the United States Navy in World War II, Korea and Vietnam. Alene was the first woman to become Rear Admiral in the United States Navy. In 1972, she was the first woman ever to be appointed to that rank. She was also the first Nurse Corps Officer assigned as Special Assistant to Assistant Secretary of Defense of Health and Environment in 1966-67. Alene was also a veteran of World War II and Vietnam.

Conclusion

As the Korean War at times has been referred to as the "Forgotten War," this is all the more reason that the stories from those who served at this time, both men and women, should not be forgotten. As we continue to follow women's journey to empowerment in the military, we cannot forget this pivotal time.

Chapter Eight
Vietnam War (1959-1975)

The Vietnam War started in 1959 when the United States made the decision to help defend South Vietnam from Communist North Vietnam. This war was vastly different from the Korean War (just six years prior) in its scope, depth, number of troops and consequently, the number of **casualties**. Therefore, medical staff, including nurses, were in high demand.

The medical evacuation of battlefield wounded was greatly improved by what the military had learned in Korea. Due to extensive use of medical evacuation helicopters, casualties were able to be treated and saved much more rapidly than in previous wars. The UH-1 utility helicopter was used by the thousands in Vietnam, and as a flying ambulance it evacuated wounded soldiers from battle areas to medical help within minutes and fifty percent faster than in Korea. Medical staff was also able to further develop triage processes and trauma care from this advanced combat medical care system.

The Vietnam War produced national protests, division, and resentment not seen before or since. On May 4, 1970, student protests at Kent State University in Ohio turned deadly when four students were shot and killed by the Ohio National Guard. And U.S. military personnel returning to the U.S. from Vietnam and overseas were often met with scorn, hostility, and rejection from their own countrymen.

Women in the Vietnam War

Vietnam happened during a difficult time in our history and society found itself in the middle of the Women's Rights Movement, as well as the Civil Rights Movement. The war was part of the internal struggle of the U.S., and women pushed past the traditional gender stereotypes from the 1950s and looked for more freedom.

Military service gave women a freedom that they may not have felt in society. Because of the large amounts of troops sent to support the massive combat operations activity in Vietnam, prejudices towards women that had previously existed were easier to overlook. In this time of a major overseas war that had not been seen since WWII, women were greatly needed to fill critical military roles and jobs.

And again, women wanted to serve. Some wanted to continue the legacy of family service, some wanted to make a difference, and some wanted excitement and adventure. Women were breaking out of the traditional roles they had been in for so long. African-American women now had more doors open to them to serve as well. They, too, found some equality in the military.

Women who chose to serve in the Vietnam War worked as nurses and other positions like news-gathering, air traffic controllers, clerks, and intelligence analysts. Just like in the past wars, civilian women did their part as well. They served in Vietnam with organizations like the Red Cross. Estimates show that 11,000 women served in Vietnam during the war.

Challenges for Women in the Vietnam War

1. Delayed service overseas.

By the Vietnam War, women had made a lot of progress on their empowerment journey into the military. So, after all of this time serving and proving themselves, did they finally see combat? Despite the constant request by women to serve in Vietnam, despite their long-standing record of dedication and service in WWII and Korea, the military decided that combat zones were not appropriate for women. Women found themselves facing the same challenge their ancestors had— apparently combat work was just not suitable for them.

Women didn't give up. They continually volunteered and requested to serve in combat areas.

By April 1965, President Johnson was sending over large quantities of troops to Vietnam. The magnitude of this war demanded the use of women. With the increase in casualties and the need to free up servicemen for combat, even the male nurses serving in hostile zones (originally thought to be too dangerous for female nurses) were not enough.

Women nurses were needed. So most women who volunteered did not serve in Vietnam until 1965.

Even once women were finally allowed to go overseas to Vietnam, the number of volunteers always outweighed the number of positions available to them. Out of the approximate 11,000 women who served in Vietnam, most were nurses.

2. Dangers while serving.

Even though women who served in Vietnam were not officially allowed to serve in combat roles, this did not mean that they escaped it. Women were exposed to many dangers while serving in Vietnam, such as incoming enemy fire directed towards U.S. installations, attacks on U.S. vehicles, aircraft crashes, and other operational hazards. As a result, eight U.S. military women were killed in Vietnam.

U.S. Air Force Captain Mary Therese Klinker was a flight nurse on the U.S. Air Force C-5A Galaxy that crashed in April 1975 near Saigon. She was serving in "Operation Babylift," a U.S. humanitarian mission to place orphans with United States families. Sadly, 138 people were killed along with Klinker and numerous children.

In 1970, WAC stenographers worked at **MACV** Headquarters in Saigon. On the way to work, the women's bus was often attacked by Viet Cong. Later, additional WACs worked in the USARV command at Long Binh Post, northeast of Saigon. Women worked long hours in high humidity, a heavy red dust, and artillery shells that even shook women from their beds. Not only did the women quickly adjust to the enemy fire, but they never asked to be transferred out of the area. The women were very dedicated to their work. They knew how important it was to the success of the war, so remained to do their jobs.

Upon returning home, both men and women felt the effects of the war. Women suffered from identical and similar mental disorders as men, like PTSD, depression, and suicide. After the war, the military did not always recognize them as having served in combat situations, especially if their service records did not formally reflect this.

Impact of Women in the Vietnam War

1. Two new uniforms for women were developed.

1960 – Two Army green uniforms were approved for women, the Army green cord suit and the Army green service uniform. Both were another step towards gender equality in the Army.

2. Met the urgent medical need.

The very large numbers of troops in Vietnam, and the high level of combat operations demanded massive medical support. Therefore, approximately 90 percent of the women who served in Vietnam were military nurses.

3. Progress towards racial equality.

Building on progress made in the Korean War, African-American women found increased opportunities to serve in combat. On July 15, 1964, Margaret E. Bailey became the first African-American nurse promoted to Lieutenant Colonel in the Army Nurse Corps.

4. Greater opportunities and advancements.

The Vietnam War clearly showed the exceptional value of women who served in the military. In 1971, women who did not have prior service experience were allowed to join the National Guard. And in August 1972, all **military occupational specialties (MOS)** were opened to WAC women, except for those that might need more training. Also, women could now command units that included men. By 1978, the number of WACs in the Army was 52,900.

Women on the Empowerment Journey in the Vietnam War

Sharon Lane (1943-1969)

Sharon Lane, of Canton, Ohio, was the only American servicewoman killed by direct enemy fire in the Vietnam War. She was assigned to the 312th Army Evacuation Hospital on April 24, 1969. While working in the Vietnamese ward, the hospital was hit by a rocket attack. As she rushed to move her patients away from the enemy fire, she was hit and killed instantly by rocket fragments. Many of her patients were saved because of her quick and selfless actions.

In this Aug. 30, 1968 photo, U.S. Army nurse Sharon Lane is promoted to First Lieutenant.

Doris "Lucki" Allen (1927-present)

Doris "Lucki" Allen, born in El Paso, TX, became the first woman full-time instructor for the U.S. Army

Doris "Lucki" Allen, later in life.

Intelligence School Interrogator Prisoner of War Course. During her tour as a senior intelligence analyst in Vietnam, her drafted intelligence report saved the lives of at least 101 Marines fighting in Quang Tri Province.

Doris "Lucki" Allen, at left, during her Army career.

> *"During my years of service I survived many prejudices against me as a woman, as a WAC, me as a soldier with the rank of specialist, me as an intelligence technician and me as a Black woman; but all of the prejudices were overshadowed by a wonderful camaraderie."*
>
> ~ Dr. Doris "Lucki" Allen

Hazel W. Johnson-Brown (1927-2011)

U.S. Army Brigadier General Hazel W. Brown,
head of Army Nurse Corps, in 1979.

Hazel W. Johnson had been told earlier in her career that she would never be able to enter a nursing program. Not only did she become Chief of the Army Nurse Corps in 1979, but she was also the first African-American woman to become Brigadier General

"Positive progress towards excellence, that's what we want…
If you stand still and settle for the status quo, that's exactly what you will have."

~Brigadier General Hazel Johnson-Brown

Conclusion

Vietnam War nurses took bold steps on their empowerment journey. They faced many of the same horrors of war as the men did. And when they came home, they experienced the same types of post-war mental disorders as men.

Women who served during the Vietnam War made significant strides towards greater equality in the armed forces, and this momentum kept them going even after the war was over.

Chapter Nine
Post-Vietnam War /Modern Conflicts (1970s—Present Day)

In the decades after the Vietnam War, the U.S. military has continued to engage in wars and conflicts. The military has sent support to natural disasters and humanitarian crises worldwide. In each of these changing missions and operations, the roles of military women were tested and continually redefined. Highlights of the over 40 years of women's service show the continued threads of the story we began with the Revolutionary War—that of women's empowerment in the military.

Changes in the military, just like in society, are happening faster than ever before. The empowerment path for women in the military is clearly marked with transformational milestones along the way. Wars are changing. Women are changing. The military is changing. And, our country is changing too.

As you read through the Transformational Milestones that follow, look for the story that emerges. What trends do you see? Where do you see equality between genders? Where do you see equality between races? What "firsts" do you see?

Transformational Milestones

October 7, 1975

President Gerald Ford signed Public Law 94-106 that allowed women to enroll in all military service academies beginning in Fall 1976.

September 1977

Basic training for men and women was consolidated.

1977

WASPs (from WWII!) were finally granted Veteran status by President Jimmy Carter.

October 20, 1978

WAC was disestablished as a separate Corps of the Army. The Women's Army Corps first opened their doors to allow women to serve in the Army back in 1943. But now, after 35 years, WAC was no longer needed because women were now integrated into the Army. All branches of the Army were open to women, except for Infantry, Armor, and Artillery, also known as the combat branches.

May 1980

Sixty-two women graduated and received a commission from West Point Military Academy.

December 1989

Operation Just Cause, Panama. Women's military roles in this crisis were critical. Captain Linda Bray, military police commander, was the first woman to command men in battle.

Two female West Point Cadets seen at their graduation in May 1980.

August 2, 1990

The Persian Gulf War (August 2, 1990 – February 28, 1991) was the largest deployment of women to a combat zone since WWII.

1994

The Direct Ground Combat Definition and Assignment Rule allowed women to be assigned to all positions that they were qualified for, except for those that would put them into direct combat.

October 6, 1997

The U.S. Postal Service officially issued a stamp honoring military women.

September 11, 2001

United States of America was attacked by terrorists. The subsequent fighting, officially called the Global War on Terror, was a significant transformation for women's military service.

The 1997 U.S. Postal Service stamp honoring women in U.S. military service.

2009

U.S. Marines first used Female Engagement Teams (FET) that worked with women in a country or area. These teams worked on building relationships and gathering intelligence.

March 10, 2010

WASPs finally receive the Congressional Gold Medal, almost 70 years after they were disbanded.

2013

Department of Defense lifted the 1994 ban on women in direct ground combat roles which opened up even more job opportunities for women, including in units that had been all men. This momentous decision to move towards integration affected the entire military, both men and women alike.

<u>All</u> **military occupation specialties** and positions opened up to women, including ground combat units, and without exception. For the <u>first time</u> in U.S. military history, women were able to contribute to the Department of Defense mission with no barriers in their way.

Today's Military Women

Today, women serve in every branch of the military. Women are in both enlisted and officer positions. Women serve in the both Reserves and Active Duty. Women serve stateside and around the world. Women are deployed. There are more than 2 million women veterans in the U.S. today. Women veterans are the nation's fastest growing veteran population. Despite all of the progress women have made, today's military women still face numerous challenges.

In Ohio alone, there are over 67,000 women veterans.

Unique Challenges for Women in Today's Military

Bias in the military.

Military women still face issues like bias and gender inferiority.

Dual roles.

Military women who are mothers feel the challenge of serving in two roles—family and the military. Women who are single parents don't always have easy access to childcare.

Access to Veterans' services and benefits.

According to the U.S. Department of Veterans Affairs, the population of female veterans is continually increasing. Services and benefits have to be available to this population of veterans.

Health.

Women who serve in Iraq and Afghanistan return home with significant health problems like traumatic brain injury and respiratory conditions. Some also face mental health conditions like PTSD, sleep disorders, and suicide. Statistics show that women in the military have higher rates of suicide than women not in the military. Overall, suicide is the second leading cause of death for U.S. service members.

Violence.

Women in the military face the threat of domestic violence and sexual assault.

Transitional difficulties – Military to Civilian life...

A woman veteran's tour ended while she was serving in Iraq. She decided not to reenlist so returned home to the United States ahead of the rest of her unit. She was excited for this new chapter in her life. When she landed at the airport, there was no fanfare to greet her and no family to welcome her with hugs and posters. They didn't live in the area. She called a friend to give her a ride home. When she got to her house, the lights were off. In her rush to get home, she had forgotten to get her utilities turned back on. She spent her first night home alone in a cold, dark house with a can of pop and a bag of chips by her side. She had been in heavy combat in Iraq just weeks before.

Soon she began to look for a job. Despite all she had learned from her military training and experience, she was continually turned down. Sometimes she heard that it was because she had seen combat and employers feared she may have PTSD. Others didn't know if she might re-enlist soon and then quit her job.

Without a steady paycheck or job, this combat veteran turned to alcohol for comfort. Her unit, which she had served so closely with for months had all chosen to reenlist so they stayed in Iraq. She was alone and ended up homeless. Thankfully, she eventually found help at a Veterans Administration Hospital.

This is just one woman's story upon returning home. While many women veterans return to a normal life after service, many have a rough transition from military to civilian life. Think back to the very beginning of this book. Who was it that you saw when you first read the word, 'veteran?' Remember, you aren't alone if you pictured a veteran who was a man. Women and men transition back to civilian life differently, just as transitions vary for each woman veteran. Women veterans feel, at times, like they are invisible simply because they don't fit the typical image of veterans that we carry in our minds.

Women veterans, like the woman in the above story, can face numerous problems when they feel "invisible." Lack of social support. Isolation. Difficulty discussing their service due to cultural norms. Homelessness among women veterans is a big concern, too.

Thanks to Veterans Hospitals and outreach programs, many women like the one who lost her home, do get help and the support they need. But many still struggle...just to be seen for who they are.

Women Continuing the Empowerment Journey

Despite the vast challenges facing today's military women, they continue to take brave steps forward and with each step, they are becoming more and more empowered in the military.

November 2, 1979 - 2nd Lieutenant Marcella Hays graduated from Army Flight school and became the first African-American female pilot in the U.S. Armed Forces.

U.S. Army Aviator Marcella Hays shown next to a UH-1H helicopter that she was trained to fly.

(50)

2000 – Captain Kathleen McGrath became the first woman to command a U.S. Navy warship.

2004 – Colonel Linda McTague became the first woman fighter squadron commander in U.S. Air Force history.

2005 – Jeanine McIntosh became the Coast Guard's first African-American woman pilot.

Jeanine McIntosh at the controls of her Coast Guard aircraft.

2005 – Sergeant Leigh Ann Hester became the first woman in U.S. military history to be awarded the Silver Star medal for direct combat action near Baghdad.

Major General Deborah Ashenhurst (U.S. Army, retired).

January 2019 - Deborah Ashenhurst became the first female Director of Ohio Department of Veterans Services (ODVS). While serving, Major General Ashenhurst was the Adjutant General and commander of the State of Ohio, and commanded 17,000 personnel of the Ohio Army and Air National Guard, Ohio military reserve and Ohio Naval militia.

Profiles of Empowered Ohio Women Veterans

Cassie Barlow (Beavercreek, Ohio)
United States Air Force

At left, Colonel Cassie Barlow seen in dress uniform (third from the left).
On right, Colonel Barlow stands at center right.

Why did you join the military?

I joined the military to get an education, through the Reserve Officer Training Corps. I loved serving and ended up staying for 26 years.

How did your civilian life prepare you for your military career?

I didn't realize it at the time, but my parents prepared me very well to serve in the military. They raised my brother and sister and I with a strong faith and values, an understanding of ethics and integrity, a commitment to serve others and a respect for the rules, while encouraging us to forge a path of our own and to not be afraid to step forward and lead.

How do you define "empowerment?"

Empowerment is giving teammates the tools they need to do their job and then standing back and watching them jump over every expectation and goal. If a leader has trust in their teammates they can accomplish anything they set their mind on.

Did you ever feel that you needed to prove yourself as a woman soldier? Why or why not?

I always put my best foot forward regardless of who was in the room with me. I learned in the military that if you were willing to jump in and contribute to the best of your ability, it didn't matter what gender or race you were. I was given a lot of opportunity to excel in the military and while I took every opportunity given, I was always looking for how I could pass that opportunity to someone else.

What rank are you most proud to have earned, and why?

My final rank of Colonel was probably the one I am the most proud of. When I began serving in the Air Force, I thought I would serve for four years and then get out of the Air Force to pursue a civilian career. I never imagined I would be in the Air Force for 26 years. I stayed in the Air Force because I loved serving and I was continually challenged with new opportunities.

Which medals or citations are you most honored to have received, and why?

The medal that I was most proud to wear was a pistol badge that I earned. It is called the Excellence in Competition Badge and means that I shot in the top 10% of competitors. This is not a badge than many get to wear, so I was very proud to have earned it and I wore it very proudly on my uniform.

What was your biggest lesson(s) learned while serving?

Diversity and inclusion are very powerful! As a kid who grew up in a very homogeneous community, it didn't take me long to figure out that inviting everyone to the table to contribute was incredibly powerful and necessary to come up with the best solutions to problems.

What is one thing you want the next generation to know or to remember about what you did while serving?

I served our country and other Airmen proudly and worked to lay the groundwork for other ladies to follow.

Barbara Cerny, (Oakwood, Ohio)
United States Army

Why did you join the military?

Long strange story. It was the fall of 1979 and if you asked me if I would join the military when I was in high school, I would have laughed you out of the county. However, never say never. I had played in the band all through junior high and high school so joined the college band in my freshman year. We had just changed to drum and bugle corps style marching and I decided to switch to being a rifle twirler. No one on campus knew anything about rifle twirling so the band director enlisted the help of the Army captain who ran the ROTC program at the college to teach us drill and ceremony. CPT Dean Kershaw had more charm in his little finger than most men have in their entire bodies and within a few weeks, all five of us girls were in ROTC. The next spring, he talked me into trying out for the Army three-year scholarship. I again laughed as I was competing against MEN for a military scholarship and no one from my little college, Mesa College, Grand Junction, CO, had ever received an Army scholarship. Lo and behold, didn't I get that scholarship! I literally sat down and put pros and cons in two columns on a paper to determine if I wanted to accept it. When I was done, the only word in the cons column was "Army". Everything else fell in the pros column. Needless to say, I accepted the scholarship and my career was born.

How did your civilian life prepare you for your military career?

My dad was a pilot in the Army Air Corps in WWII and then an officer in the US Air Force after it split from the Army. Even though he was a reservist and retired when I was just 8, he was still an influence in my decision.

What was your primary job (MOS)?

I was a Signal officer (communications).

What were your biggest challenges when you served in the military?

I had to work twice as hard as my male counterparts to be taken seriously. When the draft ended in 1973, women represented just 2 percent of the enlisted forces and 8 percent of the officer corps. Today, those numbers are 16 percent and 18 percent respectively. When I joined, women were still being kicked out if they got pregnant. I once asked a Colonel why I didn't see any field grade females in the Signal Corps headquarters at FT Gordon. His response, "You will either sacrifice the Army for your family or sacrifice your family for the Army." He would have never said that to a man. On more than one occasion, I was the only woman on maneuvers and there were no accommodations for me. I slept in the same tent, in my own corner, of course, or in the same classroom as my counterparts.

How did you get through those challenges? What helped you to work through those challenges? Who helped you to become successful and why?

I looked at the guy next to me and thought, if this idiot can do it, so can I! My biggest fans were my male bosses along the way. I had no female bosses to look up to. Many times I was not just the only female officer around, I was the only female. After my first child, I went on my two-week Reserve duty, in the field. I was pumping at the time. My female counterparts thought I was crazy but my fellow male officers called it Operation Precious Cargo, found me a cooler to dedicate to preserving my breast milk, gave me space to pump when I needed it, make sure the cooler was full of ice, and helped me get it all back without losing a drop. I loved those guys.

How do you define "empowerment?"

Let me do my job! Let your folks do theirs. An NCO, SFC White, once told me, "Ma'am, you take care of the soldier and let them take care of the mission." That is true empowerment and I live by it.

Did you ever feel that you needed to prove yourself as a woman soldier? Why or why not?

All the time. I broke my ankle once because a training officer told us women we could drop out of the obstacle course any time we wanted because we weren't strong enough. Well, I outlasted all the other women and a few of the men and fell off the last obstacle because I had nothing left in me. I won a lot of respect that day. It hurt like hell but I am still proud of that moment.

Kathleen Hayes (Shelby County, Ohio)
Women's Army Corps/United States Army

Why did you join the military?

I joined the military in 1974 in the Women's Army Corp as a WAC rank as a private and began my career starting as an Army Medic. I earned a Bachelors in Nursing degree and was then commissioned as an Army Officer which extended my nursing practice and ability to assume increased leadership. During the 35 years of service both in active duty and reserves I achieved the rank of Colonel.

How did your civilian life prepare you for your military career?

My hardworking grandparents and parents taught me at a young age the importance of God, country, respect, and a hard work ethic; this I found to be aligned with lifelong Army values.

Where did you serve?

I served in many areas; I enjoyed the humanitarian missions in South America as a nurse; during Desert Storm at Ft. Lee Virginia as a Head Nurse of Medical Surgical ward; in Egypt, as Chief Nurse of the 256th Combat Support Hospital for a 17 multi-national exercise and in Tikrit, Iraq as Chief Nurse of 345th Combat Support Hospital, where we provided full service trauma and health care to the military, to Iraqis and local nationals according to rules of war. I enjoyed working with the Iraqi Physicians and Nurses with the Trauma Care Course our Combat Support Hospital developed and taught to the Iraqi physicians and nurses to increase their level of expertise.

What were your biggest challenges in the military?

My biggest challenge was to juggle progressing up the Army leadership chain while being a wife and mother, often missing family milestones.

How did you get through those challenges? What helped you work through those challenges?

My supportive husband, family, friends and neighbors always were there to make sure our two daughters got to school, practices and sporting events. It was a collaborative network to assure success. As my daughters grew older they took an active support role, as when I was in Iraq, they organized a cookie baking team to provide care packages for our soldiers.

Who helped you to become successful and why?

Support of my husband, daughters, and friends as they maintained the home front so I could focus on the Army mission. My Army nursing leadership mentors Lieutenant Colonel Jewel Stephens and Colonel Sharon A.J. Stanley who placed me in progressive military nursing leadership positions while empowering me for success.

How do you define "empowerment?"

Servant Leadership was instrumental in my career journey. I have always valued teamwork where all members have intrinsic value beyond what they do. Leading by example in a respectful and mentoring environment allowed our military nursing personnel to provide expert health care in a combat zone. Leadership focus was always on the mission and to support the military nursing personnel in whatever they needed for career success, to include education and leadership opportunities. It was an honor to serve as an Army nurse and serve with the most respectful, professional nurse leaders who made a difference everyday in the lives of soldiers.

Margaret Kruckemeyer, (Beavercreek, Ohio) United States Army

How did your civilian life prepare you for your military career?

During my civilian nursing career, I primarily worked in military hospital/government work settings having varied assignments, like running an acute upper respiratory unit where my work assignment went from just one ward of 50 patients to seven wards of patients with same problem. This is where time management and quick physical assessment skills were developed quickly because a professional nurse was the ONLY one who administers medications.

I also married a wonderful life mate in August 16,1969, who entered the U.S. Army in 1970 to fulfill his ROTC command requirement after graduating from University of Missouri at Rolla. During our eight-year courtship, I was exposed to his military fraternity of the Pershing Rifles where he had risen to second in command prior to graduation. Both our fathers had served in World War II.

How do you define "empowerment?"

To excel in your life so to enable opportunities for yourself and others. To earn the right to be viewed as a legitimized authority for whatever field of endeavor you wish to focus on in your career. It was an honor to serve as an Army Nurse and serve with the most respectful, professional nurse leaders who everyday made a difference in the lives of soldiers.

Did you ever feel that you needed to prove yourself as a woman soldier? Why or why not?

Yes. Starting in basic training as an Army nurse, I was told that even though you may be the highest ranking officer in your unit, if you were ever captured, you would never be allowed to lead your captured group. For example, if there were only two high-ranking people, a First Sergeant and a Nurse Captain, captured with all other military members, the First Sergeant would ALWAYS be deemed the person in charge.

Up until the early 1970s or so, women in the military were never allowed to rise above the rank of Colonel despite the work abilities they proved when doing military assignments. Women seemed to feel they had to work twice as hard and prove twice as much in their accomplishments just to "stay even" with men of similar rank and military skill sets. Also, if a military woman ever got pregnant, this meant an automatic discharge, for sure. Also, military women were not to marry men that ranked higher than them because this meant an automatic discharge. Never was a woman military officer allowed to marry a male Noncommissioned Officer.

Which medals or citations are you most honored to have received, and why?

This is a sore subject for me. Women were not given the same accolades as men. For example, I was required to write up awards for male counterparts at Ft. Bragg to rise to the level of meritorious service. I, on the other hand, did three times the amount of work in the position I held for 3 ½ years and I was only awarded one Army Commendation Medal (ARCOM). I had never received an ARCOM, so was denied the Meritorious Service Medal. I was then "forced" to accept the ARCOM medal upon my discharge from active duty, and the young male Specialist next to me got the same award for doing a good job out on his six-week field assignment. In my lifetime of military service, women were not written up much back then, so in 14 years I ended up with just two ARCOMs.

My greatest award was being inducted into Ohio's Veterans Hall of Fame class of 2008.

What was your biggest lesson(s) learned while serving?

Be true to yourself and your mission in life. "Be the best you can be" at whatever job you do and find a job that needs to be done. Keep your eye on the mission/purpose and make that your work goal. If a door gets slammed in your face, know that your faith in your Lord will always help you find that open window for opportunity to continue on in your mission.

What are the top 3 things you want people to know about women veterans?

Women should be better acknowledged by their peers and others for the work they have done, starting from the Revolutionary War forward, even if rank was never granted for the work they were expected to perform. There is a place and a role for all Americans and our U.S. military is slowly coming around to this fact. Note that 12-18 percent of the various military service positions are now filled by women. Lastly, the Department of Veterans Affairs (VA) is evolving its mission care policy to increase the services to women who do have unique gender health care issues. Women veterans, like their male counterparts have EARNED THEIR RIGHT for care as stated in President Lincoln's Second Inaugural Address that has become the VA's motto: "Honor those who have borne the battle, and their widow and orphan, too."

After her military career, Margaret continued to serve as a family nurse practitioner for 33 years within the Department of Veterans Affairs, in a variety of work areas, from prime care, rehab, oncology, to hospice.

Linda Strite Murnane (Xenia, Ohio)
United States Air Force

What were your biggest challenges when you served in the military?

There weren't many women joining the service because of this very challenging requirement. Those women who did join the military and who stayed on active duty had an especially challenging time because there were no women role models or mentors. There was in many instances a specific prejudice displayed against women in the field. When I would deploy I would often be the only woman on the site. Facilities weren't adapted to have more than one gender at the site in all instances. Convincing people every day that I was at least as good or better than my male counterparts became a daily practice.

Did you ever feel that you needed to prove yourself as a woman soldier? Why or why not?

I needed to prove myself as a female airman every day of the 30 years I was on active duty. Despite the changes that occurred during my 30 years of service, there would still always be a few people who were convinced that women didn't belong in the military.

What was your greatest accomplishment while serving?

I had a lot of them. The fact that I went from an Airman Basic and retired as a Colonel and Chief Circuit Judge was a pretty amazing feat. The fact that I completed law school in two and one-half years, while having two babies born while in law school, graduating with honors and passing the bar exam on first attempt during that time was also pretty amazing. Being selected to be on the first U.S. Military Assistance Team (MAT) to go to Rwanda after the genocide was pretty amazing. Presiding at the first U.S. Air Force trials in the area of operations during Operations Iraqi and Enduring Freedom was pretty amazing.

Which medals or citations are you most honored to have received, and why?

The Legion of Merit. It is an award that is ranked above a Distinguished Flying Cross. It entitles the individual who earns it to be buried in Arlington National Cemetery, and while I don't really want to be buried in Arlington National Cemetery, the fact that I performed service that qualifies me for that honor is something of which I am quite proud.

What did you go on to do after your military service?

Upon retirement I spent about one year as a felony prosecutor in a small rural county in Ohio. I was then selected to serve as the Executive Director of the Kentucky Commission on Human Rights, leading a team of more than 20 people responsible for investigating and prosecuting civil and human rights violations in 118 counties in Kentucky. I left that position to work for the United Nations first as the Senior Legal Officer in the Trial Chamber trying individuals most responsible for war crimes, crimes against humanity and genocide. After two years in that position I accepted a position as the Senior International Attorney for the U.S. Defense Institute for International Legal Studies managing and supervising global support teams conducting human and civil rights training around the globe.

After one year in that position I returned to work for the United Nations as the Chief, Court Management Services at the International Criminal Tribunal for the former Yugoslavia (ICTY). My assignments at the ICTY were in The Hague, The Netherlands. I worked three years in that position, and then returned to the U.S. where I spent one year as a judicial bailiff working for The Honorable Anne Taylor at the Franklin County, Ohio, Municipal Court in Columbus, Ohio. At the end of one year on Judge Taylor's team, I returned to the United Nations as the Chief, Court Management Support Services at the Special Tribunal for Lebanon, located in Leidschendam, The Netherlands. I returned from that position in May 2017, and accepted a position working for Lexis Nexis in Miamisburg, Ohio and am now working as a legal researcher for Western Governors University.

What was your biggest lesson(s) learned while serving?

Be self-reliant -- depend on yourself to achieve your goals. Don't accept failure. If you don't succeed the first time you try, prepare, work harder, and try again. Never give up. Never give up. Never give up. It's never too late to succeed.

What is one thing you want the next generation to know or to remember about what you did while serving?

I would like the next generation to know how difficult it was for women to succeed -- intentionally or unintentionally there were obstacles everywhere you turned. While there were a few good men willing to treat you as an equal, for the most part everyone assumed you were inferior from the moment you walked in the door -- or sometimes even before you walked in the door -- that is, as soon as they saw you were a woman by looking at your name on an assignment order. And what I would like the next generation to know is that all of those assumptions people made about me were wrong -- and to keep that in mind when you judge people before giving them a chance to prove themselves.

What are the top 3 things you want people to know about women veterans?

We endured tremendous obstacles in our pathways to success. We also served -- and did so with distinction. We are proud of our service to our nation.

Karen Nagafuchi (Fairborn, Ohio)
United States Air Force

Why did you join the military?

I grew up in a small town with a father that was a P.O.W. in World War II and a brother who died shortly after returning from Vietnam. It seemed natural to join the military and serve the country. I was very interested in seeing the rest of the country and seeking adventure as well as having a career I could be proud of.

What was your primary job (MOS)?

In my 30-year military career I was a Flight Nurse, Chief Nurse and Squadron Commander. I flew Aeromedical Evacuation with the C-130 and C-9 missions, was a Standardization and Evaluation Chief and Chief Nurse with the C-9 mission, was a Chief Nurse of an Aeromedical Staging and Transport Squadron and a Medical Squadron, and a Commander of a Medical Squadron.

How do you define "empowerment?"

The equal opportunity and the ability to progress if I choose without the bias usually seen in the general public. Knowing that you can choose to make decisions with the consequence of only your decision and not the fact that you made one.

Did you ever feel that you needed to prove yourself as a woman soldier? Why or why not?

I believe that I was self-motivated to accomplish my goals. I believed in proving women as equal competitors and encouraged others to do the same.

What rank are you most proud to have earned, and why?

Colonel is the rank that I am most proud of. It is a difficult rank that only a very small percentage achieve. It includes great responsibility as well as great opportunity to help others achieve their goals.

What was your biggest lesson(s) learned while serving?

The biggest lesson learned while serving is to do what is right and to treat everyone with respect. Work hard to bring out the very best in people.

What is one thing you want the next generation to know or to remember about what you did while serving?

Next generation: You go into the military for a purpose and an ideal of the military that is honorable and patriotic. You believe in the cause, knowing there is hardship at times and that it is the right thing to do.

What are the top 3 things you want people to know about women veterans?

Women are a valuable asset to the military. Women are frequently humble about their military service.

Robin Titus (Dayton, Ohio)
United States Navy

Why did you join the military?

I joined to serve this great nation, but primarily to have my degree and educational costs paid for.

Where did you serve?

I was a Reserve Component Member; my tours included La Maddalena, Italy, London, UK, and Kuwait. My Active Duty tour from 2009-2010, was in Kuwait.

What were your biggest challenges when you served in the military?

Serving in leadership roles and positions as a female. Many times, I was overlooked due to my gender and more importantly because of my race. It was not typical in the 90s to see an African-American female in my position as Trainer, and ultimately trying to reach the rank of Chief Petty Officer.

How did you get through those challenges?

Endured, trained harder, worked diligently with the Navy Knowledge online training modules to make myself marketable and the go-to for programs and services. I learned what any female would do to make themselves more visible.

What helped you to work through those challenges?

My work ethics and values instilled in me to win. Continuing the drive to succeed; and to bring those up behind me who have similar desires and wants.

Who helped you to become successful and why?

Many leaders who have crossed my path. I went in at 33, therefore I was at a mature age and knew pretty much what I wanted to accomplish. Being mature helped to steer my decision making.

How do you define "empowerment?"

The ability to give strength to self and to others, while feeling the power of success; and to help them feel confident enough to pay it forward.

Did you ever feel that you needed to prove yourself as a woman soldier? Why or why not?

A female sailor, yes. Because it was hammered into our brains, that we were not equal to our male counterparts. However, the internal strength and my wisdom is what I tried hard to display, especially when I was at the policy-making and decision-making tables.

What was your greatest accomplishment while serving?

Making the rank of Chief Petty Officer of the Navy.

Which medals or citations are you most honored to have received, and why?

JSAM - Joint Service Achievement Medal; because this medal shows you were effective and did exceptional work at a Joint Command: Navy, Army, Air Force, etc.

What are the top 3 things you want people to know about women veterans?

We are given equal jobs and opportunity now, we are respected, and we are responsible for having made decisions like women on ships, on submarines. Women are in higher ranks now such as Admirals, and Fighter Pilots. We are finally considered equal participants in service to this great country.

Chapter Ten
Concluding Thoughts on Empowerment

Our nation has two million women veterans and each one of them has a story. That's a lot of stories in our history and many of those have disappeared over time. It is up to us to continue to tell the story of our women veterans. To sit down to talk with them about their service. To find out what they did. To understand the sacrifices they made and the ongoing struggles they went through in order to serve. We are the ones who will benefit in tremendous ways. Just as these women in history empowered each other, their stories also empower us. They empower us to take the next steps. To become stronger and more confident. To take risks. To go after our dreams.

What these women did was to live life the way they wanted to—with courage and self-determination. Every time a woman persevered, she was taking yet another step towards empowering herself and other women, even those she would never meet.

It took our country awhile to learn how to best use military women to their fullest potential. As the military evolved, the positive impact of women on the mission or the war became more and more evident. Women in the military have made immeasurable contributions to protecting our freedoms. And they will continue to do so.

How can we remember to see women veterans for who they really are? How can we see all that they have done for our country? We can start by recognizing the numerous women of the past who fought—not only for our country, but also for *who* they wanted to be. At times, women were steered into certain positions rather than being allowed to choose their own path. Despite these barriers, women continued to push forward and make sacrifices.

Women hid in men's uniforms in order to serve in the Revolutionary and Civil War. Women serving as WASPs did not wear uniforms in World War II. Women were not always seen for who they were or what they could contribute. And yet they knew they had a place in the military, uniforms or not.

Women faced numerous difficulties. Despite not always being recognized for their sacrifices or service; they didn't give up. They continued to lead a courageous path for other women to follow.

It's time that we remember. It's time that we see the vast contributions made by women in the military, in whatever way that they served. It's time that we see the women, themselves. It's time that we see the woman veteran at the fast-food counter, and in the parade. Stories of women's patriotism and sacrifice are all around us.

We see them. We recognize them. And we thank them.

Several female Vietnam veterans visit Ft. Lee, Virginia.

The Class of 2020 at the U.S. Military Academy at West Point learn their military assignments for the next step in their military careers.

RESOURCES FOR FURTHER LEARNING AND STUDY

Ohio Veterans Hall of Fame

Located in Columbus, Ohio, the Ohio Veterans Hall of Fame recognizes the veterans' military accomplishments and community service. Of the 895 Ohio veterans inducted, there are 67 women veterans in the Ohio Veterans Hall of Fame. To learn more about these women, follow the link below and then click on the woman's name you wish to learn about.

www.ohiovet.gov/main/women-veterans-Ohio-Vets-HOF.html

Lynn Ashley, U.S. Army, Class of 1999
Cassie Barlow, U.S. Air Force, Class of 2018
Jennifer Baun, U.S. Navy, Class of 2015
Anna Beall, U.S. Army, Class of 2013
Lynn Black, U.S. Army, Class of 1994
Betty Brown, U.S. Army, Class of 1999
Dorothy Budacki, U.S. Navy, Class of 2005
Blanche Aviles Casey, U.S. Air Force, Class of 2017
Dorothy Cornelius, U.S. Navy, Class of 1997
Margaret Delillo-Storey, U.S. Army, Class of 2011
Alene Duerk, U.S. Navy, Class of 1999
Laura Williams Dunlop, U.S. Army, Class of 2003
Charity Earley, U.S. Army, Class of 1993
Rebecca Eden, U.S. Army, Class of 2008
Sallie Farmer, U.S. Army, Class of 1994
Florence Fawley, U.S. Marines, Class of 2001
Phyllis Fitzgerald, U.S. Air Force, Class of 2009
Nada Fleming, U.S. Navy, Class of 2008
Esther Frazier, U.S. Navy, Class of 1996
Ruby Gilliam, U.S. Navy, Class of 2014
Mary Glover, U.S. Army, Class of 2011
Anna Gray, U.S. Navy, Class of 1997
Susan Green, U.S. Army, Class of 2016
Mary Gruber, U.S. Marines, Class of 2014
Brook Harless, U.S. Army, Class of 2017
Mary Hanna, U.S. Air Force, Class of 2019
Sara Harper, U.S. Marines, Class of 1993
Linda Hart, U.S. Navy, Class of 2011
Kathleen Hayes, U.S. Army, Class of 2012
Elaine Tisdel Herrick, U.S. Air Force, Class of 2014
Edith Doctor Jobe, U.S. Army, Class of 2003
Kelly Knox, U.S. Army & Air Force, Class of 2016
Holly Koester, U.S. Army, Class of 2017
Margaret Kruckemeyer, U.S. Army, 2008
Barbara Ann Krzewinski, U.S. Navy, Class of 2003
Sharon Lane, U.S. Army, Class of 1995

Ellen Leidy, U.S. Marines, Class of 2007
Frona Liston, U.S. Navy, Class of 2017
Audrey Mackiewicz, U.S. Coast Guard, Class of 1995
M. Jean Madden, U.S. Army, Class of 1999
Opal McAlister, U.S. Army, Class of 2007
Helen McClelland, U.S. Army, Class of 1995
Martha McCrary, U.S. Army, Class of 1996
Mary McHugh, U.S. Navy, Class of 2012
Janice Messenheimer-Courtney, U.S. Army, Class of 2015
Lois Nelson, U.S. Army, Class of 1995
Nora Noble, U.S. Air Force, Class of 1996
Katherine Platoni, U.S. Army, Class of 2019
Elva Pounders, U.S. Marines, Class of 2008
Doris Powell, U.S. Army, Class of 2009
Mary R. Powell, U.S. Army, Class of 2009
Dana Robinson-Street, U.S. Navy, Class of 2018
Bonnie Rost, U.S. Navy, Class of 2000
Barbara Rounds, U.S. Army, Class of 2000
Lauretta Schimmoler, U.S. Army, Class of 1993
Linda Spoonster Schwartz, U.S. Air Force, Class of 2004
Nancy Sherlock, U.S. Air Force, Class of 1994
Sharon Stanley, U.S. Army, Class of 2013
Bobbie Stern, U.S. Army, Class of 1997
J. Lori Stone, U.S. Air Force, Class of 2019
Mary Stout, U.S. Army, Class of 1994
Kathryn Sullivan, U.S. Navy, Class of 2001
Josephine Trotter, U.S. Navy, Class of 2006
Betty Stagg Turner, U.S. Air Force, Class of 2005
Debborah Wallace, U.S. Army, Class of 2016
Sunita William, U.S. Navy, Class of 2001
Freda Winning, U.S. Marines, Class of 1995

Ways to Honor and Remember Our Women Veterans

1. March is Women's History Month.

      Pick a time in women's history that you would like to learn more about. Several museums and organizations plan events to honor women during this special month. Find an event in your town that will highlight women's history, struggles and achievements, such as your local library or a museum. Look into programs in your community as well as online.

2. June 12th has been designated as Women Veterans' Day in Ohio. Other states acknowledge this day as well.

      What is one thing you can do to honor and thank women on Women Veterans' Day? Where can you find women veterans to thank?

3. Remember that Veteran's Day is different from Memorial Day. And, remember that Armed Forces Day is different from both of those days as well.

      How do each of the days differ from the other? Mark all three days on your calendar. List different activities you can do to honor the appropriate people on the appropriate day.

4. Veteran's Oral History

      Find a woman veteran in your area. Interview her about her service, what she learned from that time and how she was changed by her service to our country. Ask her about what empowerment means to her and how her time in service impacted her life.

Women veterans of World War II saluting at a ceremony at the Veteran's National Cemetery in California.

Women's Military Memorials & Museums

Spanish-American War Nurses Memorial, Arlington National Cemetery, Arlington, VA

World War II Memorial, Washington, D.C.

This memorial remembers WWII servicemen's and women's contributions to the nation.

Korean War Memorial, Washington, D.C.

This memorial's statues portray male soldiers in the field, while the black granite
wall backdrop includes women embossed in the background.

Ohio Korean War Veterans Memorial and All Veterans Walkway, Dayton, Ohio
This memorial honors the significant contributions of men and women in the armed forces
during the Korean War.

Sharon Lane Memorial at Aultman Hospital, Canton, Ohio
This is one of the first Vietnam memorials made in the United States, and it was to honor
a fallen woman soldier. The names of 110 Stark County servicemen (and one woman)
who died in the Vietnam War are written on the base of the memorial.

Vietnam Veterans Memorial and Vietnam Women's Memorial, Washington, D.C.
The Vietnam Veterans Memorial honors the men and women who served in the Vietnam War,
and chronologically lists the names of 58,318 Americans who gave their lives for our country.
The Vietnam Women's Memorial provides a place of healing for women veterans who served.

Did you know that there are also Vietnam women veterans' names included on
the Wall? Eight women veterans listed who lost their lives while serving in
Vietnam.

1st Lt. Sharon Ann Lane
2nd Lt. Pamela Dorothy Donovan
Lt. Col. Annie Ruth Graham
Capt. Mary Therese Klinker

2nd Lt. Carol Ann Elizabeth Drazba
2nd Lt. Elizabeth Ann Jones
Capt. Eleanor Grace Alexander
1st Lt. Hedwig Diane Orlowski

The Women in Military Service for America Memorial

Located in Washington, D.C., The Women's Memorial honors the service of America's women in defense of the nation from the founding of the country to the present.

National Women's History Museum

Located in Alexandria, Virginia, the National Women's History Museum preserves and shares the powerful history of women in America.

Bibliography

Lexico Dictionary Online, from https://www.lexico.com/definition/empowerment

Cambridge Dictionary Online, from https://dictionary.cambridge.org/us/dictionary/english/empowerment

A Life and Character Peculiarly Distinguished: Deborah Sampson in the Revolutionary War – https://ohiomemory.ohiohistory.org/archives//3520

Women in Battle in the Civil War – www.socialstudies.org

Ohio and Cleveland's role in the Civil War recognized on 150th anniversary year – www.cleveland.com/metro/2011/04/ohio_and_clevelands_role_in_th.html

Women Amidst War – https://www.nps.gov/articles/women-amidst-war.htm

Female Soldiers in the Civil War – https://www.battlefields.org/learn/articles/female-soldiers-civil-war

Women Soldiers of the Civil War – https://www.archives.gov/publications/prologue/1993/spring/women-in-the-civil-war-1.html

Women and the Spanish-American War – https://womhist.alexanderstreet.com/teacher/spanishamerican.htm

Notable African-American military women veterans – https://connectingvets.radio.com

The Hello Girls: America's First Women Soldiers by Elizabeth Cobbs

Brief History of Black Women by Kathryn Sheldon, former curator, Women in Military Service For America Memorial Foundation, Inc. – https://www.womensmemorial.org/history-of-black-women

Breakthroughs for Black Military Women – https://www.womensmemorial.org/breakthroughs-military-women

Ohio History Center

The History of Wartime Nurses, Duquesne University – https://onlinenursing.duq.edu/history-wartime-nurses/

America's Patriotic Victory Gardens – https://www.history.com/news/americas-patriotic-victory-gardens

1939-1945 – Women in the US Army

The Angels of Bataan and Corregidor: 70 Years Later, Voices from the Past

The Role of Women in the Korean War – https://koreanwarlegacy.org/chapters/the-role-of-women-in-the-korean-war/

Women in the Korean War Era – https://www.womensmemorial.org/collection/detail/?s=women-in-the-korean-war-era

Women veterans mark 60th anniversary of Korean War - https://www.army.mil/article/75736/women_veterans_mark_60th_anniversary_of_korean_war

Women Who served Their Country During the Korean War: A Tribute to the Female Patriots Who Made Contributions and Sacrifices to the War Effort in Korea – www.koreanwar-educator.org/topics/women_in_korea/women_in_korea.htm

American Military Women – The Journey Continues by Judith Bellafaire, Ph.D., Curator, Women in Military Service For America Memorial Foundation, Inc. https://www.womensmemorial.org/americas-military-women

Highlights in the History of Military Women – https://www.womensmemorial.org/timeline

Ohio Veterans Hall of Fame

Women Marines called into action to support Korean War efforts - Celebrating 100 years of women in the Marine Corps - https://www.quantico.marines.mil/News/News-Article-Display/Article/1666069/women-marines-called-into-action-to-support-korean-war-efforts-celebrating-100/

1960s: Vietnam – https://www.womensmemorial.org/history/detail/?s=1960s-in-vietnam

The Women's Army Corps during the Vietnam War by Colonel (Ret.) Bettie J. Morden

Women in the Vietnam War – https://www.history.com/topics/vietnam-war/women-in-the-vietnam-war

Vietnam Women veterans, What you may not know - https://www.army.mil/women/history/

Why Women Veterans are 250% More Likely Than Civilian Women to Commit Suicide", August 15, 2019, by Kate Henricks, Thomas & Kyle Hunter, Military Times

Disabled American Veterans, "Women Veterans: The Long Journey Home" (Sept. 2014)

U.S. Department of Veterans Affairs, "America's Women Veterans" (Nov. 2011)

U.S. Military Lifts Ban on Women in Combat by Sarah Pruitt – https://www.history.com/news

Learning Activities

A. Vocabulary Matching Exercise

Match each definition to the right word by writing the correct letter in the space.
Use the words in parentheses to help you look in the right chapter(s) for help.

1. ____ Veteran
2. ____ Veterans Day
3. ____ Empowerment
4. ____ Camps (Rev., Civil)
5. ____ Camp Follower (Rev., Civil)
6. ____ Rations (Rev., WWII)
7. ____ Social Norms (Rev., Civil)
8. ____ Soldiers Aid Societies (Civil)
9. ____ ANC (Spanish-American)
10. ____ Medal of Honor (Civil)
11. ____ Casualty (Vietnam)
12. ____ Victory Gardens (WWI, WWII)
13. ____ Women's Armed Services Integration Act (WWII)
14. ____ Soldiers Home (WWII)
15. ____ POW (WWII)
16. ____ Honorable Discharge (Rev.)
17. ____ WAC (WWII)
18. ____ Switchboards (WWI)
19. ____ Demobilize (WWII, Korea)
20. ____ WAVES (WWII)
21. ____ WAC (WWII)
22. ____ MOS (Modern)
23. ____ Transformational Milestones
24. ____ Military ID Card
25. ____ MACV (Vietnam)

a. Prisoner of War
b. Army Nurse Corps
c. A system of medical care for veterans.
d. A federal holiday to honor military veterans, those who have served in the U.S. Armed Forces.
e. Mission Occupational Specialty, a specific job in the military
f. Women's Army Corps
g. The process of gaining confidence in oneself and in taking steps to reach a goal.
h. A piece of equipment used that connected phone calls made to and from a certain place.
i. Organizations that supported the troops by raising money, getting food and medical supplies.
j. Gave women permanent status in the military, including veterans benefits.
k. Women who left their homes to follow the Army camps of their husbands.
l. U.S. Military Assistance Command
m. A person who has served in the military.
n. The nation's highest military honor.
o. The acceptable behavior that a person is to conform to in a society or culture.
p. To be released from military service.
q. Women Accepted for Voluntary Emergency Service
r. Official identification that verifies proof of current or past military service.
s. Women's Army Corps
t. A certain amount of an item, for example—food, given to each person.
u. Discharged from military service with an honorable record.
v. Home vegetable gardens that provided food for families, to not tax food supplies for soldiers.
w. Where the military lives while serving.
x. A military person lost through death or injury.
y. A significant event that changes someone's life.

B. Essay Questions – For Reflection

1. Compare and contrast the Revolutionary War and the Civil War with World War I. What are the biggest differences in women's empowerment? Why do you think women gained the opportunities that they did in World War I? Provide examples from your reading.

2. Choose a woman that you learned about from one of the early wars (Revolutionary War through World War II) and then select one from the *Profiles of Empowered Ohio Women Veterans* section. What similarities do you see in their struggles? What similarities do you see in women's empowerment? Pretend that the two women you selected could meet in person today. Write out three questions each would like to ask the other. Then write out how they each might answer those questions. What could they learn about each other by asking those particular questions? How might what they learn from each other be helpful in their own empowerment journey?

3. Select an aspect or quality of empowerment that you feel is the most difficult (for example, having to tackle the same barrier over and over again). Using examples from the reading, why is that particular aspect or quality of empowerment so difficult? Highlight a particular woman from the reading that stood out to you. How do you think she was able to push through her challenges, regardless of how hard they were?

C. Special Project - Design a Veterans Memorial

At the end of this book, you will find a listing of various Veterans Memorials throughout the country (including Ohio!).

Reflect on the military memorials that you, personally, have visited or have heard about.

How many of them honor both the military service of men and women? Are the images on the memorial typically men or women? Why do you think that memorials may not always give equal design space to all groups of people, including women? Do you agree that women should have their own separate memorials or should they be included with men? Why or why not?

Part One:
Do some research in your hometown. Does it have a memorial to veterans? If so, does it honor a specific war or all wars? Does it include both men and women? Learn what you can about why the memorial was originally created, what it took to raise the money for such a project, and what the memorial dedication was like.

Part Two:
After reading this book and the stories of the military women through history, if you could create a new memorial in your town that would honor military women, what would that memorial be? Write up a description of your new memorial including: which war(s) it honors, why you selected that war and the women who served in it, and what you want people to know about those women. What lasting message would you want people to remember after they visited your memorial?

Part Three:
Think about what the design for your memorial would look like. Oftentimes, memorials break the traditional mold and something entirely different is created. Using a pencil, colored pencils or markers, sketch out your memorial's design and be sure to leave room for writing on it. Make sure the memorial includes who-what-where-when-why.

_____
_____
_____
_____
_____
_____
_____
_____
_____
_____
_____
_____

Vocabulary Matching Exercise

Answer Key

1. M Veteran
2. D Veterans Day
3. G Empowerment
4. W Camps
5. K Camp Follower
6. T Rations
7. O Social Norms
8. I Soldiers Aid Societies
9. B ANC
10. N Medal of Honor
11. X Casualty
12. V Victory Gardens
13. J Women's Armed Services Integration Act
14. C Soldiers Home
15. A POW
16. U Honorable Discharge
17. F WAC
18. H Switchboards
19. P Demobilize
20. Q WAVES
21. S WAC
22. E MOS
23. Y Transformational Milestones
24. R Military ID Card
25. L MACV

NOTES

Download free teachers guides at www.chpsbooks.org/teacher-guides

Special discounts for Schools/Teachers and Group/Wholesale orders are available. Please contact 937-643-0502 or chps@woh.rr.com for more information.

Made in the USA
Monee, IL
07 September 2023

42256057R00044